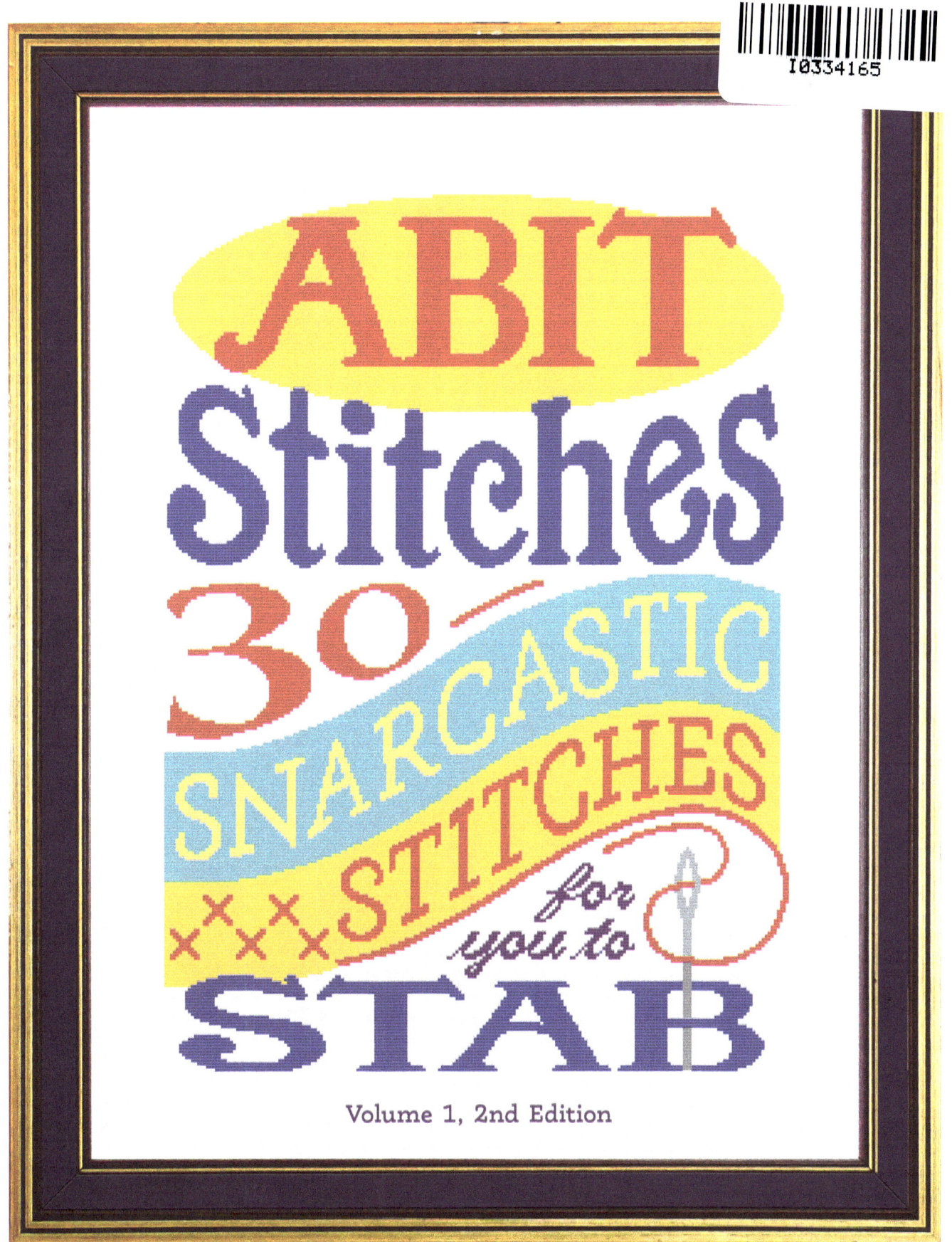

A BIT Stitches

30 Snarcastic Stitches for you to STAB

Volume 1, 2nd Edition

by Tara K. Reed & Roy W. P. Reed
with art by Erin Bennett

The Reed Studio   DOORFLOWER COMPANY

Tara and Roy definitely deserve a high-five for their brilliant execution of a stitched neon sign AND their understanding of where french fries fall on the priority list! **ABIT Stitches** lets you take a nice, constructive stabbing break anytime too much becomes WAY too much!

—*Haley Pierson-Cox, author of Improper Cross-Stitch, Cross Stitch The Golden Girls, and Feminist Stitches*

Copyright © 2022 Doorflower Company/The Reed Studio

All rights reserved. This book and any portion thereof may not be reproduced in any manner whatsoever without the express written permission of the publisher. It is prohibited to copy any part of this book for the purposes of sharing or selling.

ISBN: 978-0-9937812-7-8

Tara@doorflowercompany.com
TheReedStudio@gmail.com

Dedicated to our mother, Helen, the Queen of HEARTS.

Roy and Tara would like to acknowledge Natasha's and Nathane's patience, Helen's perseverance, Erin's creativity, and Jen's advice.

Welcome to ABIT Stitches Volume 1!

Years ago, my (much) older brother, Roy, started telling me to "write that down!" when I made him laugh. A bunch of those jokes made it into my interactive romantic comedy novel, Love Him Not, but I still found myself with quite a quantity of quality quips and nowhere to quirk. It was a real... quagmire.

Master-crafter that he is, Roy--who ruins Secret Santa for everyone but the person whose name he draws—said, "We should turn them into cross-stitches!"

Admittedly, I scoffed at the idea. You see, I was our family's latch-hook kid. My fingers were deemed too "tiny" and "dangerous" to wield a needle while my family got to stab things repeatedly and with reckless abandon. Wallowing in deep resentment of my stitching siblings' digital dexterity, I turned my back on crafts. So I had no idea there was a long history of smart people sewing subversive sass, let alone a 21st-century resurgence of the art-form's popularity! Full of good ideas, that Roy.

In the years since he started designing the patterns for this book, I learned to stitch (Victory is mine!) and have really come to love it! I've also watched the stitching community grow with so many incredibly talented and creative designers that I worried there might not be room for us. (And then I got over it, and here we are!) Cross-stitch books are everywhere these days so we appreciate you spending your coins on this one.

As winner of my high school's 'Most Sarcastic Female' award, probably too much of my self-confidence rides on whether you find ABIT to be an hysterical addition to this glorious bandwagon. If you like it as much as we hope you will, you can also thank our sister, Erin, who leant her artistic flourish to many of the patterns, and our mother, Helen, who deftly stitched most of the finishes presented here and on our online store. If you don't like the book, you can blame them as well—we plan to! Until we know your verdict, we'll set to work on Volume 2.

Ready. Set. Stab!

Tara K. Reed
Doorflower Company

Table of Contents

Using This Book 71
Catalogue 01
Patterns 33
How-To 73

Always a Godmother	05....32	I'm Not Off-Kilter	18....56
Be a Little More Hard to Get	02....38	It's Okay to Rationalize	19....68
Be the Change I Want to See	07....34	Just Fries. No guys	22....42
Carpe Do'em	03....39	Passive Aggressive	16....49
Climb Every Mountain	09....36	Pick All the Battles	24....53
Eat, Pray, Loathe	23....40	P. S. I Loathe You	29....67
Go Flaunt Yourself	01....44	Repiphany	30....58
Grant Me the Serenity	06....46	Revenge is the Best Revenge	25....57
He's Just One Guy	27....41	Sarcasm is a Condiment	20....59
I Do All My Own Stuntmen	17....48	Sascrotch	08....64
I Need a Little Blue Pill	10....43	Swearing is Part of My Charm	04....62
I Only Get Better With Rage	13....54	Thank You for Being a Fiend	26....31
If You Love Something	14....52	Truly, Truly, Truly Outraged	15....60
I'll Be the Death of You	12....45	Until I Get the Blue Box	11....55
I'm an Emotional Eater	21....50	You're Next	28....66

Be sure to read Using This Book to take full advantage
of the catalogue details and chart features.

If you've got it...take it somewhere else.

Beginner
Pg 46
9 ½" x 6 ¾"/ 24 x 17cm
Aida: 13" x 10"/ 33 x 25.4cm
Frame: 12" x 9"

This is a very muted, antique-looking design. For something more modern, substitute the pastels with intense or bright colours.

Like disinfectant wipes.

Intermediate
Pg 40
7 ¼" x 7"/ 18.4 x 17.8cm
Aida: 11" x 11"/ 28 x 28cm
Frame: 8" x 8"

You can increase the contrast between the letters and the cactus by using darker greens. Use your favourite colour for the flower.

Seize the lay!

Beginner
Pg 41
7 ¾" x 6 ½"/ 19.7 x 16.5cm
Aida: 12" x 10"/ 30.4 x 25.4cm
Frame: 10" x 8"

If you want some variety, try different colours of flowers. The black border can be changed to match any frame or room decor.

The reigning Ms. Congenifuckingality.

Intermediate
Pg 64
7 ¾" x 5 ¾"/ 19.7 x 14.6cm
Aida: 12" x 10"/ 30.4 x 25.4cm
Frame: 10" x 8"

Add more jewels or take some away. Use a metalic silver or gold thread and stitch the entire crown using just that colour.

Bibbity, Boppity, Boo, you whore.

Intermediate
Pg 34
10 ¼" x 7"/ 26cm x 17.8cm
Aida: 14" x 11"/ 35.6cm x 28cm
Frame: 12" x 9"

You might like to switch the colours around. Make a purple wand with pink letters, for example. Substitute the darks for darks and the lights for lights.

Also, a really durable roll-up carpet and some duct tape would be great.

Advanced
Pg 48
7 ½" x 7 ½"/ 19 x 19cm
Aida: 11" x 11"/ 28 x 28cm
Frame: 10" x 10"

Any bright colour will stand out against the dark brown soil if you want to play with the flowers. Likewise, try other colour combos for the lettering.

Start with your outfit.

Beginner
Pg 36
8" x 10"/ 20.3 x 25.4cm
Aida: 12" x 14"/ 30.4 x 35.6cm
Frame: 9" x 12"
Do you have a big stash of floss? Every letter could be a different colour. Or you can reign the craziness in by making each word a single colour.

Advanced
Pg 66
9" x 11"/ 22.9 x 28cm
Aida: 13" x 15"/ 33 x 38.1cm
Frame: 10" x 13"

Match your decor by changing the purple packaging to another dark hue, or swap out the underwear colours for something more 'you.'

Keeping new-relationship virginity intact with every missed bikini wax.

Fighting is one of my favourite things.

Advanced
Pg 38
6 ½" 8"/ 16.5 x 20.3cm
Aida: 10" x 12"/ 25.4 x 30.4cm
Frame: 8" x 10"

Feeling playful? Change the colour of the girl's dress, shoes, and hair. Put her in jeans and give her a haircut if you want.

It might help me with my heart-on.

Beginner
Pg 45
6 ¼" x 4"/ 15.9 x 10cm
Aida: 10" x 8"/ 25.4 x 20.3cm
Frame: 8" x 6"

Mix in some pink hearts with the blue to add variety to the design. Make sure to use a light and a dark pink to keep the shadow effect.

Bitchfest at Tiffany's.

Intermediate
Pg 57
8 ¼" x 5 ½"/ 20.9 x 14cm
Aida: 12" x 9"/ 30.4 x 22.9cm
Frame: 10" x 8"

If you'd like to make the words stand out, go with a darker blue. Make the diamonds shine more by using a deep blue in the border.

Can't say I didn't warn you.

Intermediate
Pg 47
6 ½" x 5"/ 16.5 x 12.7cm
Aida: 10" x 9"/ 25.4 x 22.9cm
Frame: 8" x 6"

Backstitching a black outline on DEATH will make the word really stand out. Pull it all together with a black rectangular border edge.

And it doesn't get any better than this.

Beginner
Pg 56
5" x 4"/ 12.7 x 10cm
Aida: 9" x 8"/ 22.9 x 20.3cm
Frame: 7" x 5"

If you're up for the challenge, try adding a third or fourth red tone to RAGE by using medium-dark rows in the middle and very-dark rows at the bottom.

If it comes back to you, it's weak too.

Beginner
Pg 54
7 ½" x 7 ¾"/ 19 x 19.7cm
Aida: 12" x 12"/ 30.4 x 30.4cm
Frame: 10" x 10"

This design would look just as stunning using a single colour for all the lettering. You can emphasize the birds by using a contrasting colour.

*My rage is contagious.
Truly, truly, truly contagious.*

Advanced
Pg 62
9 ½" x 6 ¾"/ 24 x 17cm
Aida: 13" x 10"/ 33 x 25.4cm
Frame: 11" x 8 ½"

Need more sparkle? Add more stars. Or, play with the star colour pairs. Try purple and pink, or pink and orange for a few.

Part of my active lifestyle.

Advanced
Pg 51
8" x 5"/ 20.3 x 12.7cm
Aida: 12" x 9"/ 30.4 x 22.9cm
Frame: 10" x 8"

We recommend you use black aida cloth to eliminate all the black fill stitches in the middle. Use three strands of black floss if you use white cloth.

*Crash, bang, boom.
Emphasis on the "bang."*

Advanced
Pg 50
8 ½" x 5 ¾"/ 21.6 x 14.6cm
Aida: 12" x 9"/ 30.4 x 22.9cm
Frame: 10" x 8"

Want to add a personal touch? Customize the colour of the boxer shorts and the other items blasting out of the explosion.

TARA K. & ROY W. P. REED   17

And I'm fresh out of whack.

Intermediate
Pg 58
7 ½" x 6 ½"/ 19 x 16.5cm
Aida: 11" x 10"/ 28 x 25.4cm
Frame: 10" x 8"

Use any colours you want for the lettering.
Raid your stash of thread and go bananas.

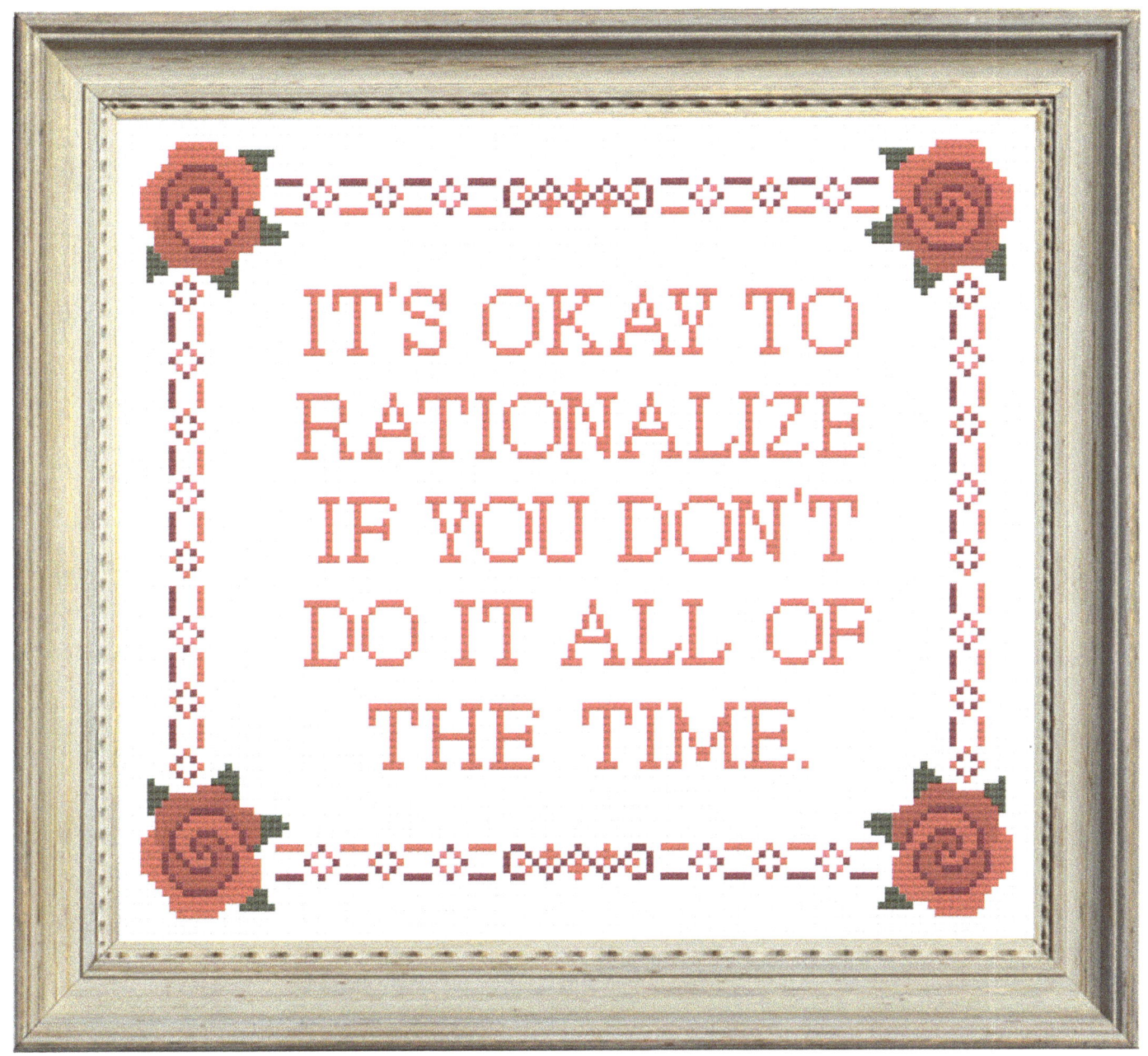

The mean is justified in the end.

Intermediate
Pg 70
9" x 7 ½"/ 22.9 x 19cm
Aida: 13" x 11"/ 33 x 28cm
Frame: 10" x 8"

Make the lettering stand out more with a darker colour choice. Emphasize the diamond border by using just one colour.

With relish!

Beginner
Pg 61
5 ½" x 3 ½"/ 14 x 9cm
Aida: 9" x 7"/ 22.9 x 17.8cm
Frame: 7" x 5"

Switch around the colours. Change the ketchup letters to mustard and the relish to ketchup.

Like, I don't even care if they're not keto.

Intermediate
Pg 52
9 ½" x 7 ½"/ 24 x 19cm
Aida: 13 ½" x 11 ½"/ 34.2 x 29.2cm
Frame: 11" x 8 ½"

Personalize this design by swapping out the pink and purple with new colours. Make sure to use a light and a dark so the check pattern stands out.

Or, as we (should) say in Canada, "Only poutine for this poutain."

Intermediate
Pg 44
4 ¾" x 5" / 13 x 12.7cm
Aida: 9" x 9"/ 22.9 x 22.9cm
Frame: 6" x 6"
The coloured paper in the tray can be changed to a muted green to contrast with the red lettering. Pale blue squares will make the fries pop.

Not necessarily in this order.

Beginner
Pg 42
4 ¾" x 5 ¼"/ 12 x 13cm
Aida: 8" x 9"/ 20.3 x 22.9cm
Frame: 6" x 6"
You can affect the overall feel by changing the colour scheme. Make it moodier with deeper hues. Lights become mediums. Mediums become dark.

Take all the prisoners!

Intermediate
Pg 55
6 1/2" x 6 1/2"/ 16.5 x 16.5cm
Aida: 10" x 10"/ 25.4 x 25.4cm
Frame: 8" x 8"
Look at flags for other colour schemes. Canada would be red and white, for example.

Serving vengeance realness!

Beginner
Pg 59
5 ½" x 5 ½"/ 14 x 14cm
Aida: 9" x 9"/ 22.9 x 22.9cm
Frame: 6" diameter hoop/ 6" x 6"

Medium green letters will stand out against the red bleeding hearts and match the yellow bird's foot trefoils—the flower of revenge.

Travel down to hell and back again.

Intermediate
Pg 33
8 ¼" x 6"/ 20.9 x 15.2cm
Aida: 12" x 10"/ 30.4 x 25.4
Frame: 11" x 8 ½"

Emphasize the sinister by using the same grey-green for all the leaves, and use the FIEND colours for all the lettering.

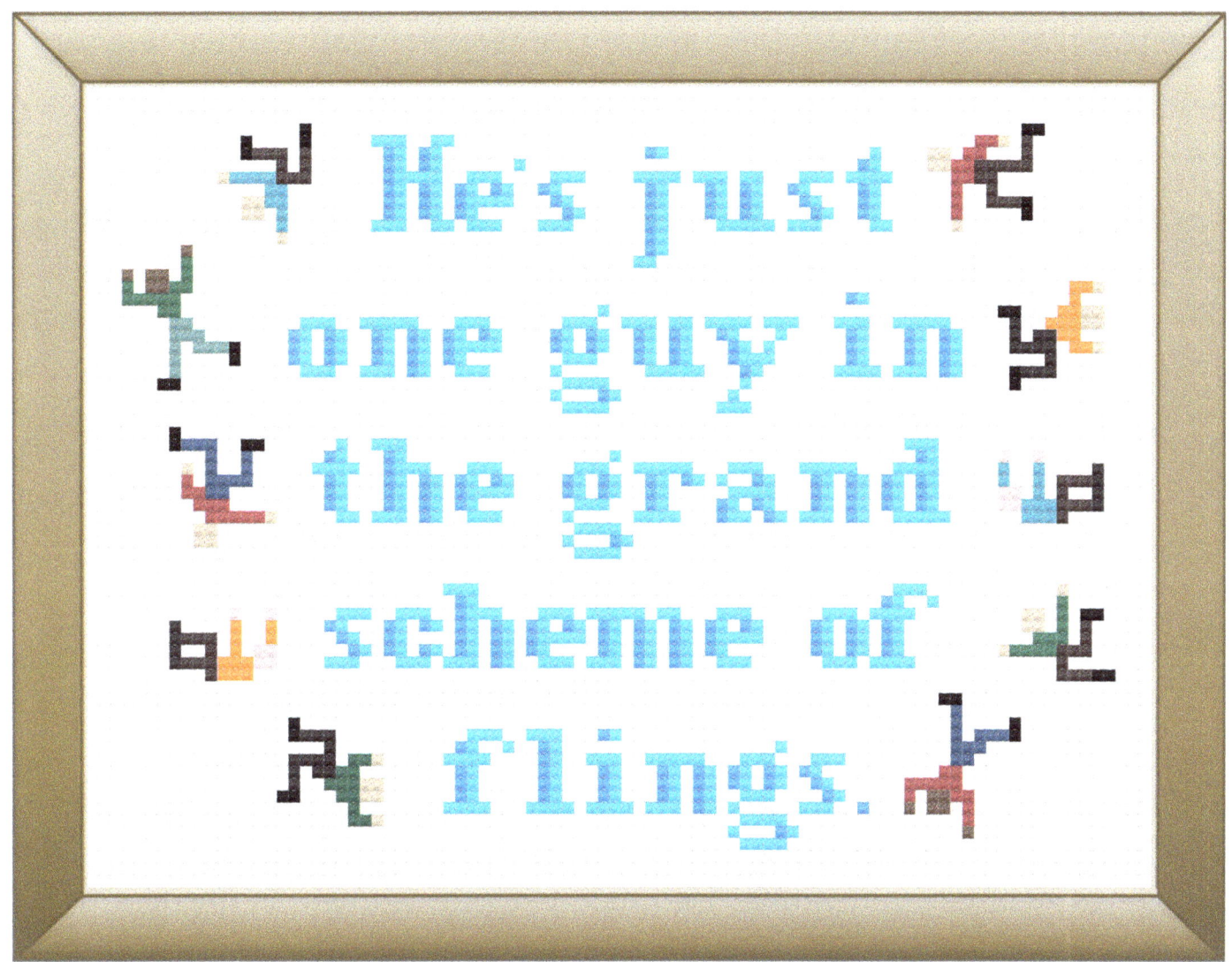

Fling. Flang. Flung.

Beginner
Pg 43
6" x 4 ½"/ 15.2 x 11.4cm
Aida: 10" x 8"/ 25.4 x 20.3cm
Frame: 8" x 6"

You have free reign for the colours in this pattern. Just make sure to use a dark and a light for the letters so you don't lose the shadows and depth.

But probably not last.

Intermediate
Pg 68
6 ¼" x 4"/ 15.9 x 10cm
Aida: 10" x 8"/ 25.4 x 20.3cm
Frame: 8" x 6"

Flip through a fashion magazine to pick new letter colour combinations that match the current style trends.

P.P.S. Die!

Beginner
Pg 69
7 ½" x 6"/ 19 x 15.2cm
Aida: 11" x 10"/ 28 x 25.4cm
Frame: 10" x 8"

Try some other pastel combinations to customize the border design. Use a monochrome or contrasting colour scheme.

Having the same great idea twice.

Beginner
Pg 60
7 ½" x 6 ½"/ 19 x 16.5cm
Aida: 11" x 10"/ 28 x 25.4cm
Frame: 10" x 8"

Using an off-white or antique aida cloth colour will make the light bulbs pop and play up the effect of "paper" that the dictionary definition is printed on.

TARA K. & ROY W. P. REED 31

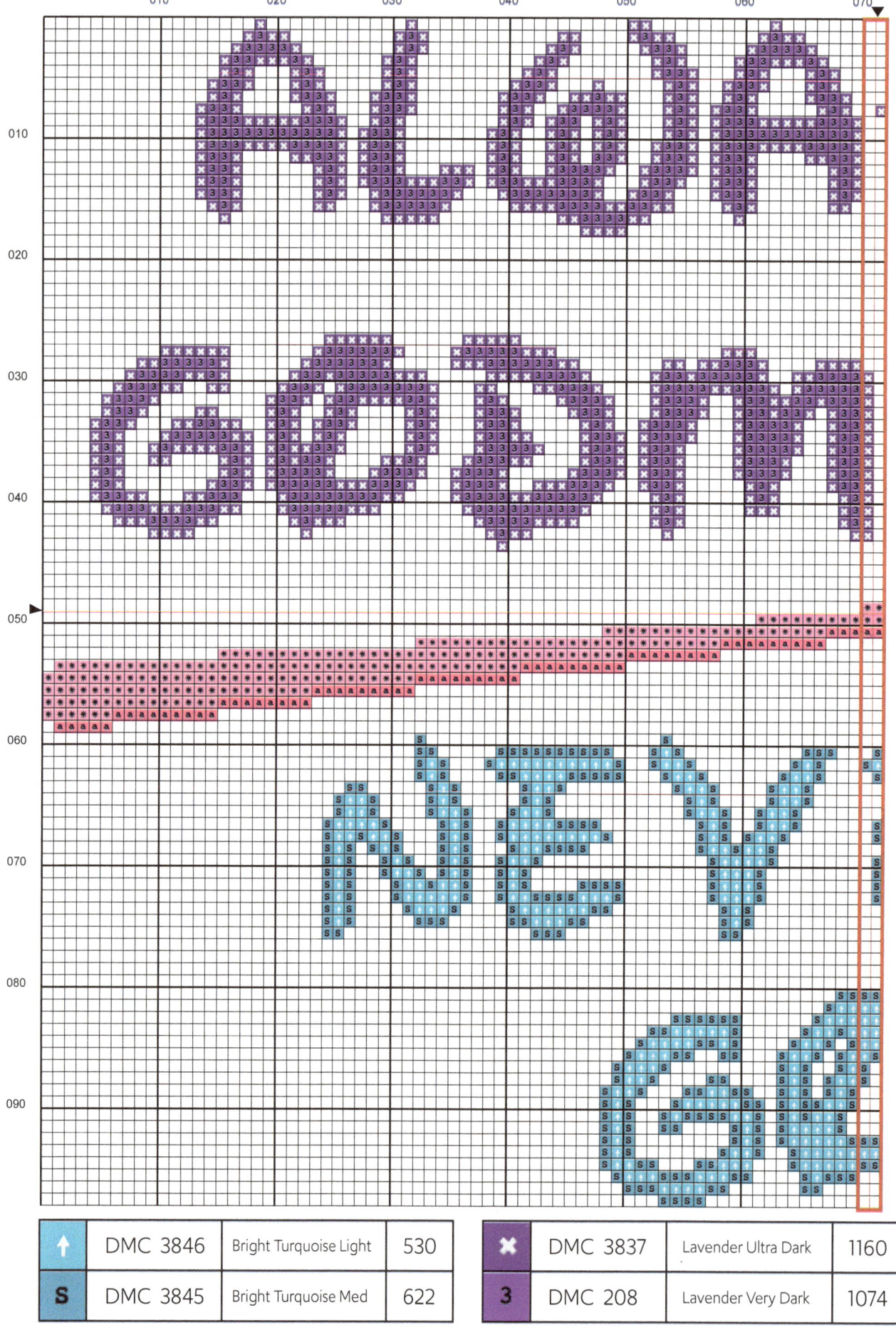

>	DMC 444	Lemon Dark	496
*	DMC 605	Cranberry Very Light	253
a	DMC 603	Cranberry	101

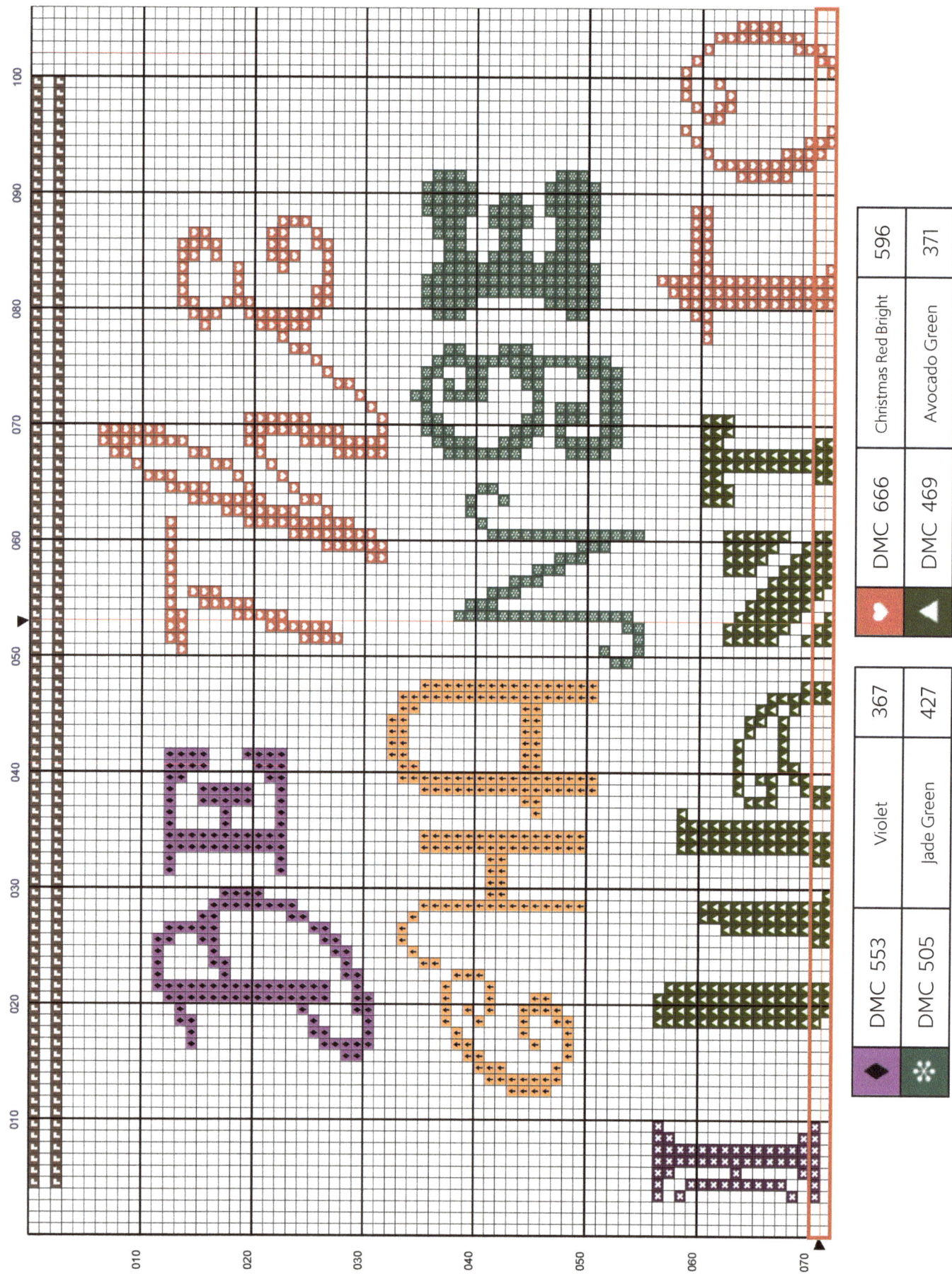

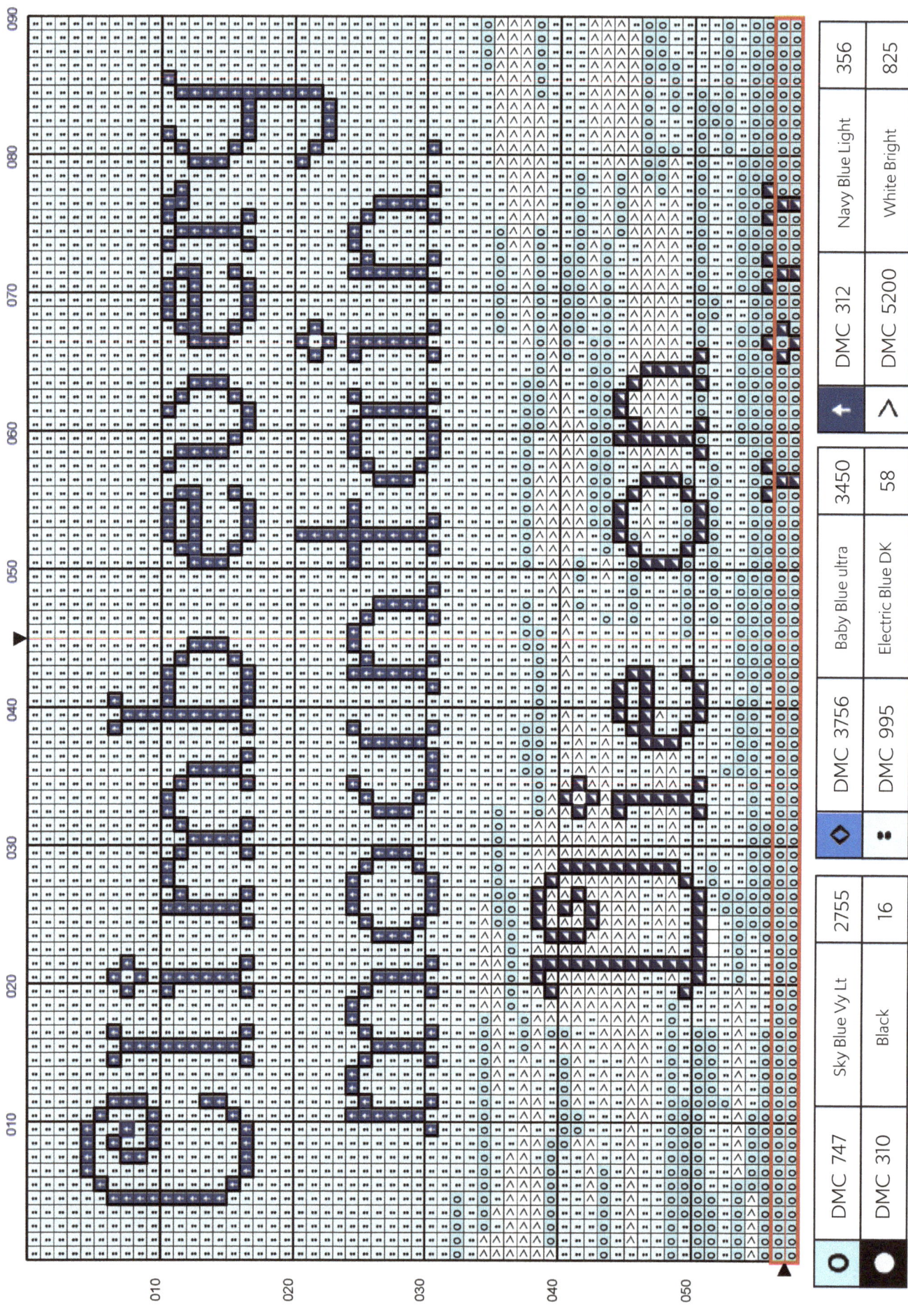

Red sections overlap–stitch only once.

	61	Autumn Gold Lt
	17	Autumn Gold Med
☐	DMC 3855	
❯	DMC 3854	

	36	Flesh Ultra Vy Lt
	1167	Hunter Green Med
H	DMC 3770	
S	DMC 3346	

	7	Golden Brown DK
	890	Parrot Green Lt
✖	DMC 975	
‖	DMC 907	

TARA K. & ROY W. P. REED 37

	DMC 699	Christmas Green	4090		DMC 3818	Emerald Green Ultra	757
S	DMC 907	Parrot Green Light	382	▲	DMC 3853	Autumn Gold Dark	227
✳	DMC 3855	Autumn Gold Light	444	O	DMC 712	Cream	596
a	DMC 603	Cranberry	65	⧗	DMC 838	Beige Brown Very Dark	171

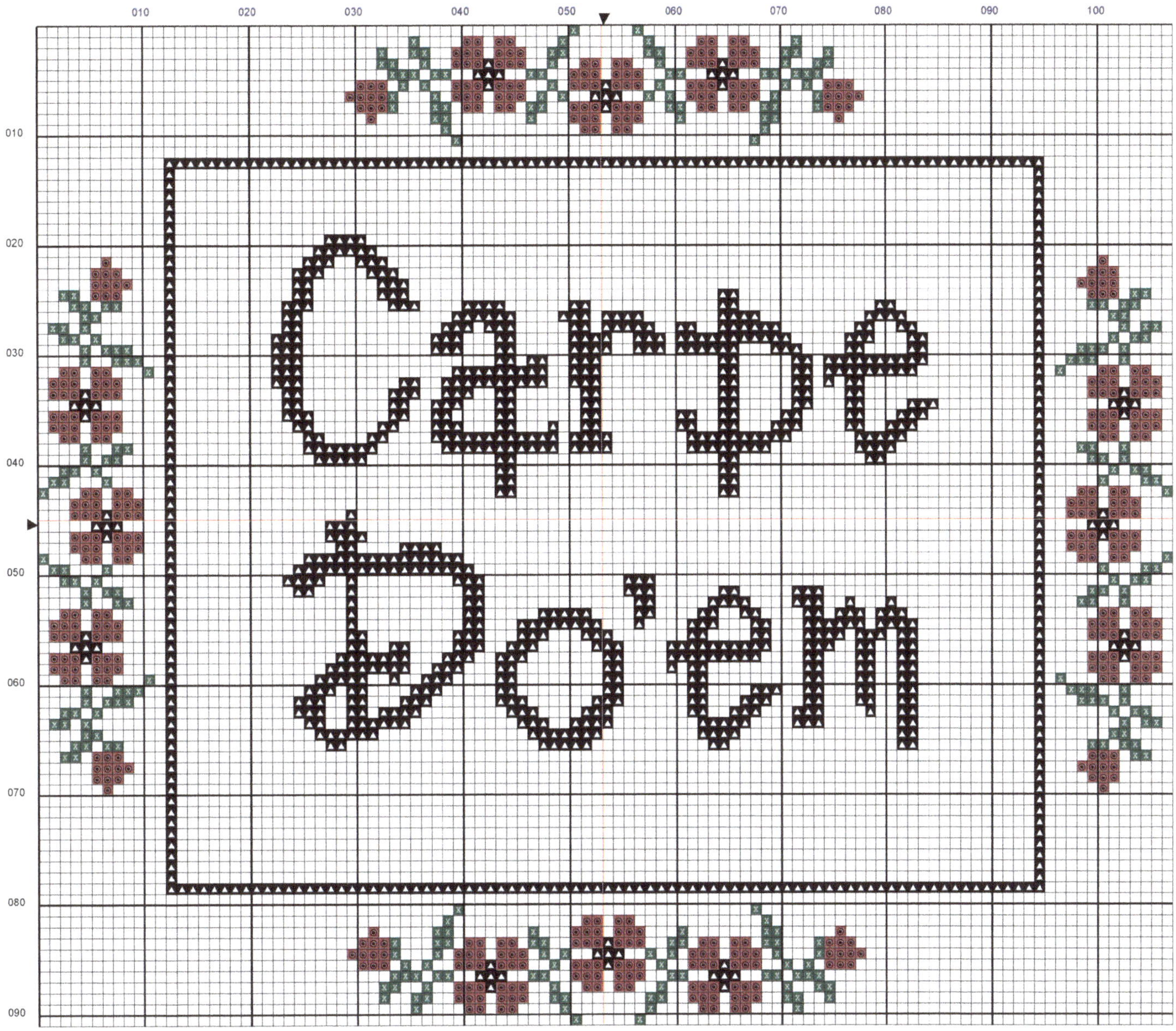

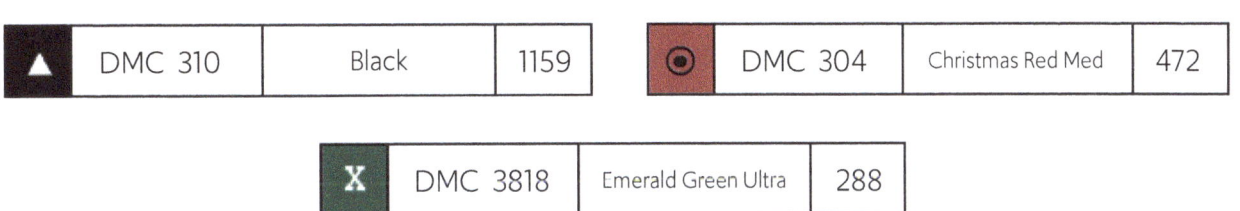

▲	DMC 310	Black	1159	⊙	DMC 304	Christmas Red Med	472
				X	DMC 3818	Emerald Green Ultra	288

TARA K. & ROY W. P. REED

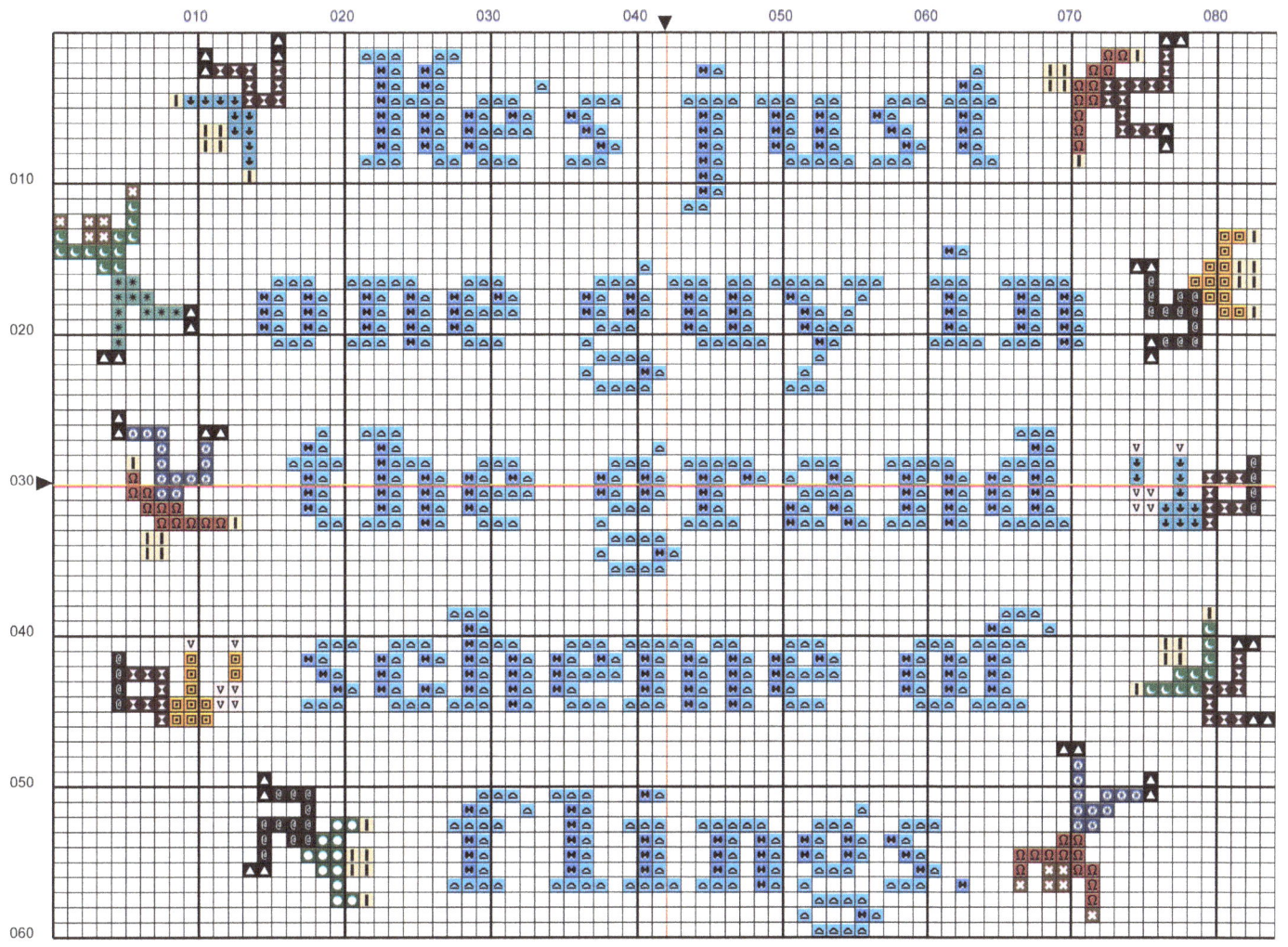

⋈	DMC 995	Electric Blue Dk	201
✪	DMC 3842	Wedgewood Dk	24
↓	DMC 3844	Bright Turquoise Dk	21
◠	DMC 996	Electric Blue Med	541
✻	DMC 3849	Teal Green Light	11
☾	DMC 699	Christmas Green	22
●	DMC 3818	Emerald Green Ultra	12
▣	DMC 741	Tangerine Med	23

Ω	DMC 3831	Raspberry Dk	34
▲	DMC 310	Black	32
∣	DMC 739	Tan Ultra Light	36
V	DMC 818	Baby Pink	12
✕	DMC 838	Beige Brown Vy Dk	47
@	DMC 3371	Black Brown	32
✗	DMC 3862	Mocha Beige Dk	12

TARA K. & ROY W. P. REED

	DMC 728	Golden Yellow	263
	DMC 744	Yellow Pale	377
	DMC 3832	Raspberry Med	438

	DMC 666	Christmas Red Bright	316
	DMC 3371	Black Brown	170
	DMC 3865	Winter White	374

ABIT Stitches

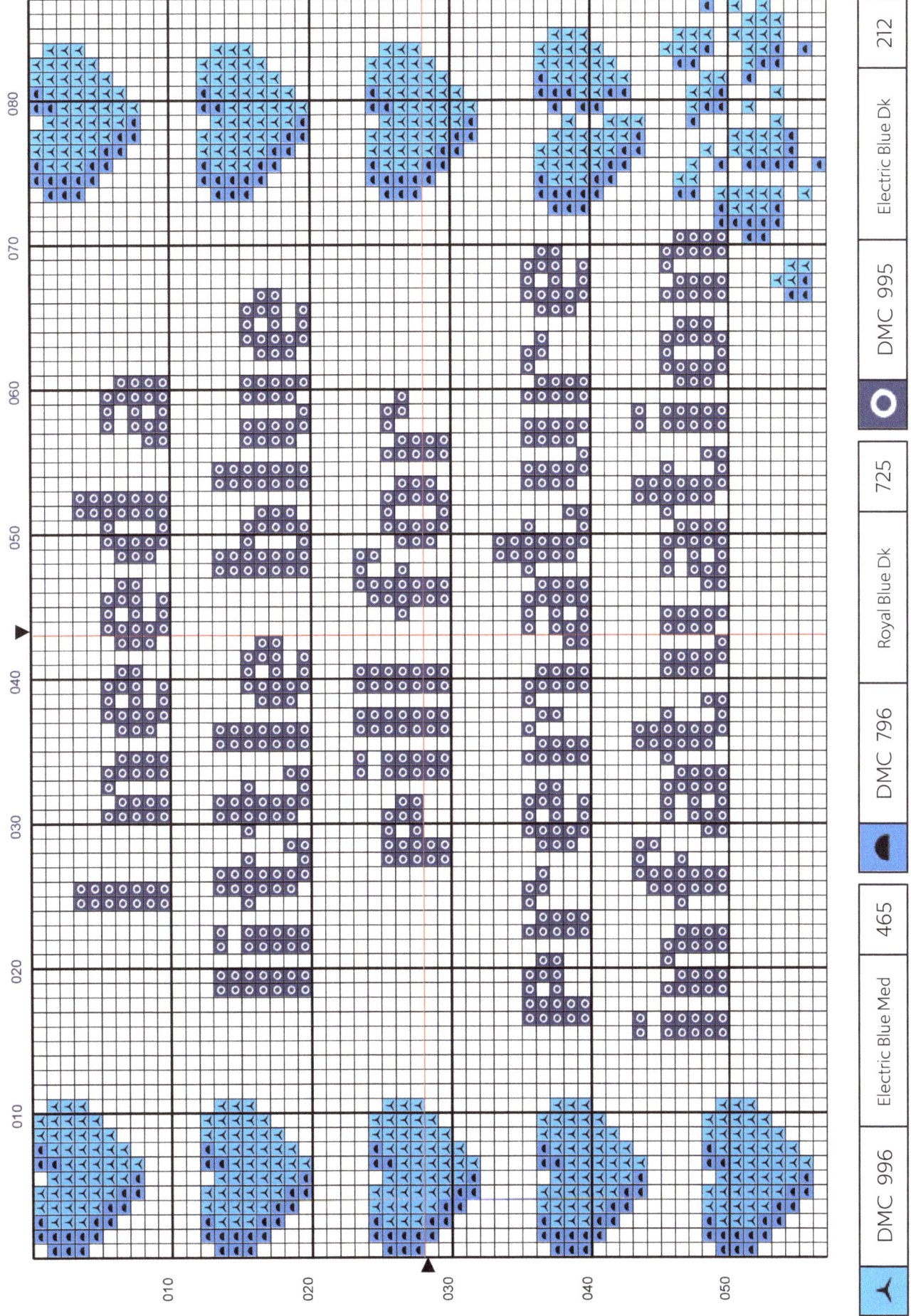

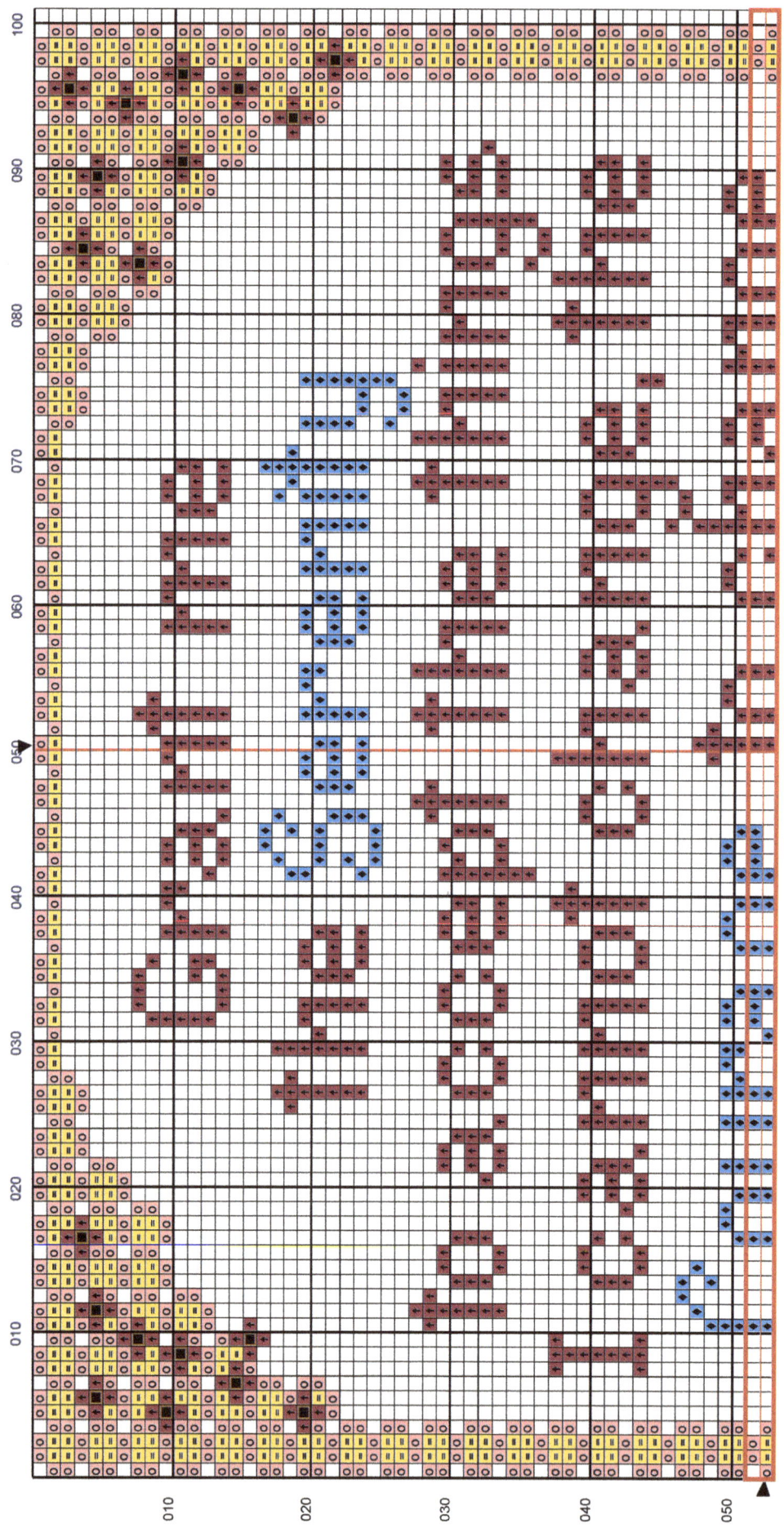

46 ABIT Stitches

Red sections overlap-stitch only once.

	DMC 782	136	Topaz Dark
●	DMC 318	60	Steel Grey Light

	DMC 434		Brown Light
★		312	

TARA K. & ROY W. P. REED

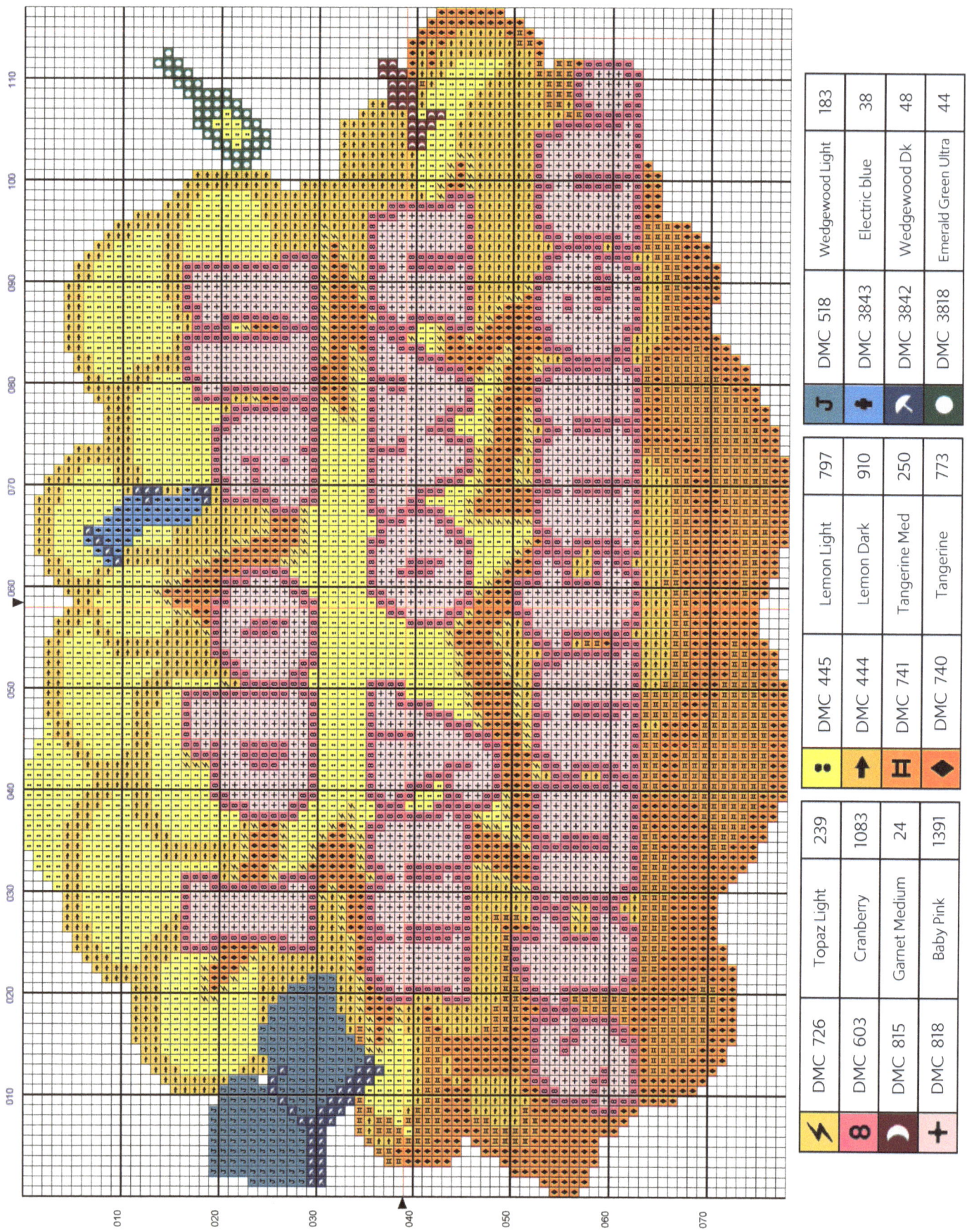

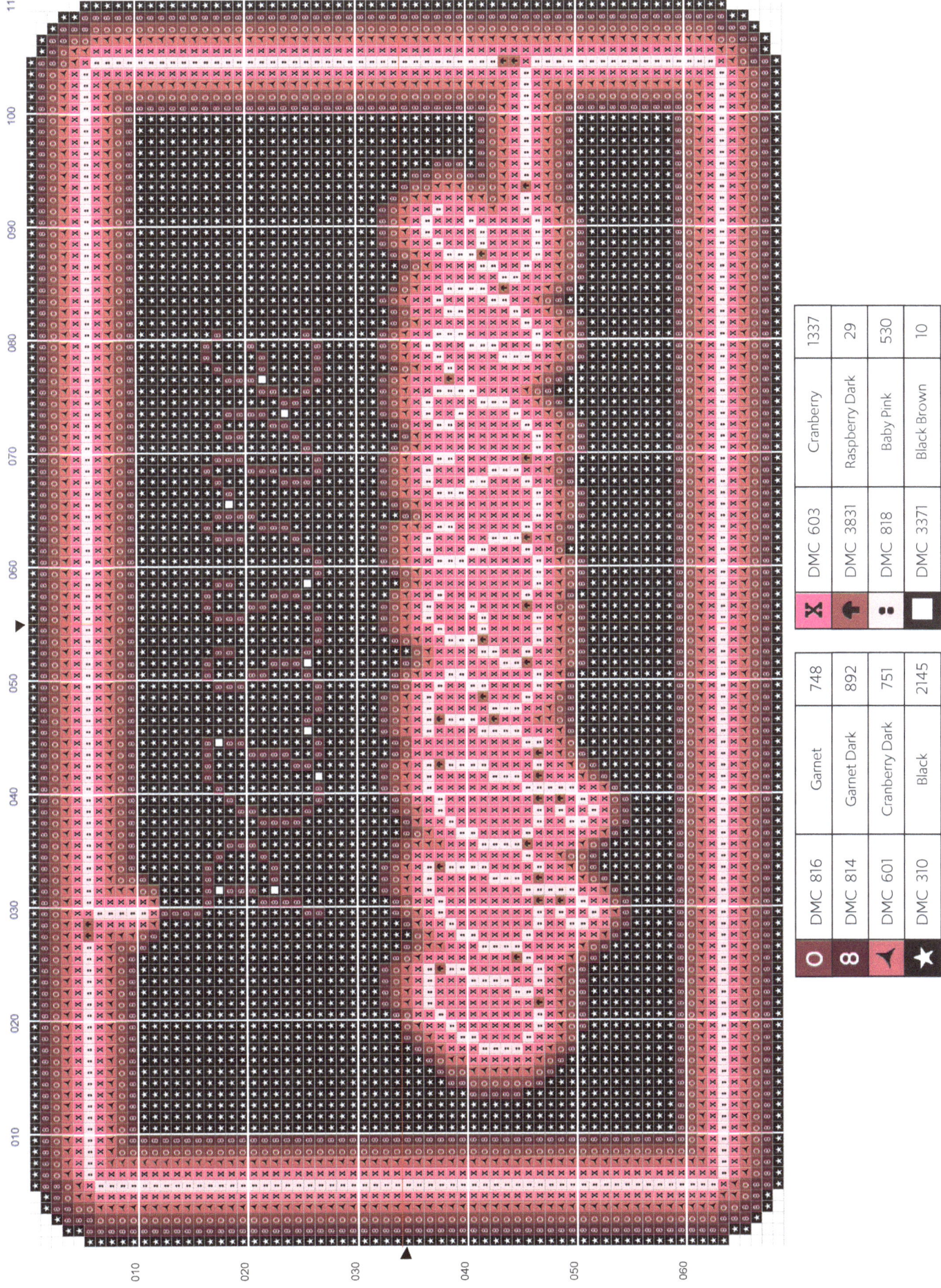

TARA K. & ROY W. P. REED

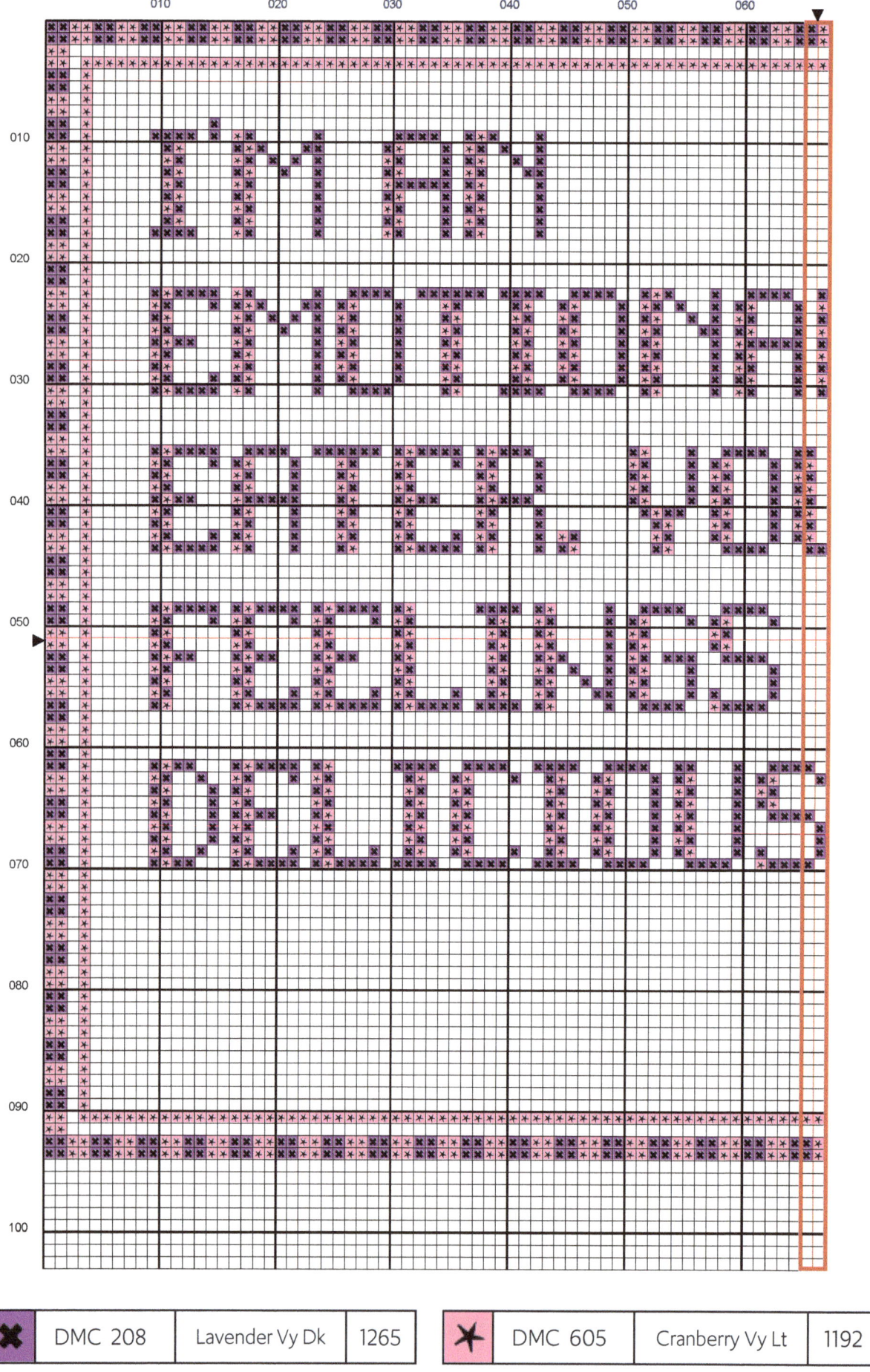

↑	DMC 415	Pearl Grey	847
○	DMC 414	Steel Grey Dk	582

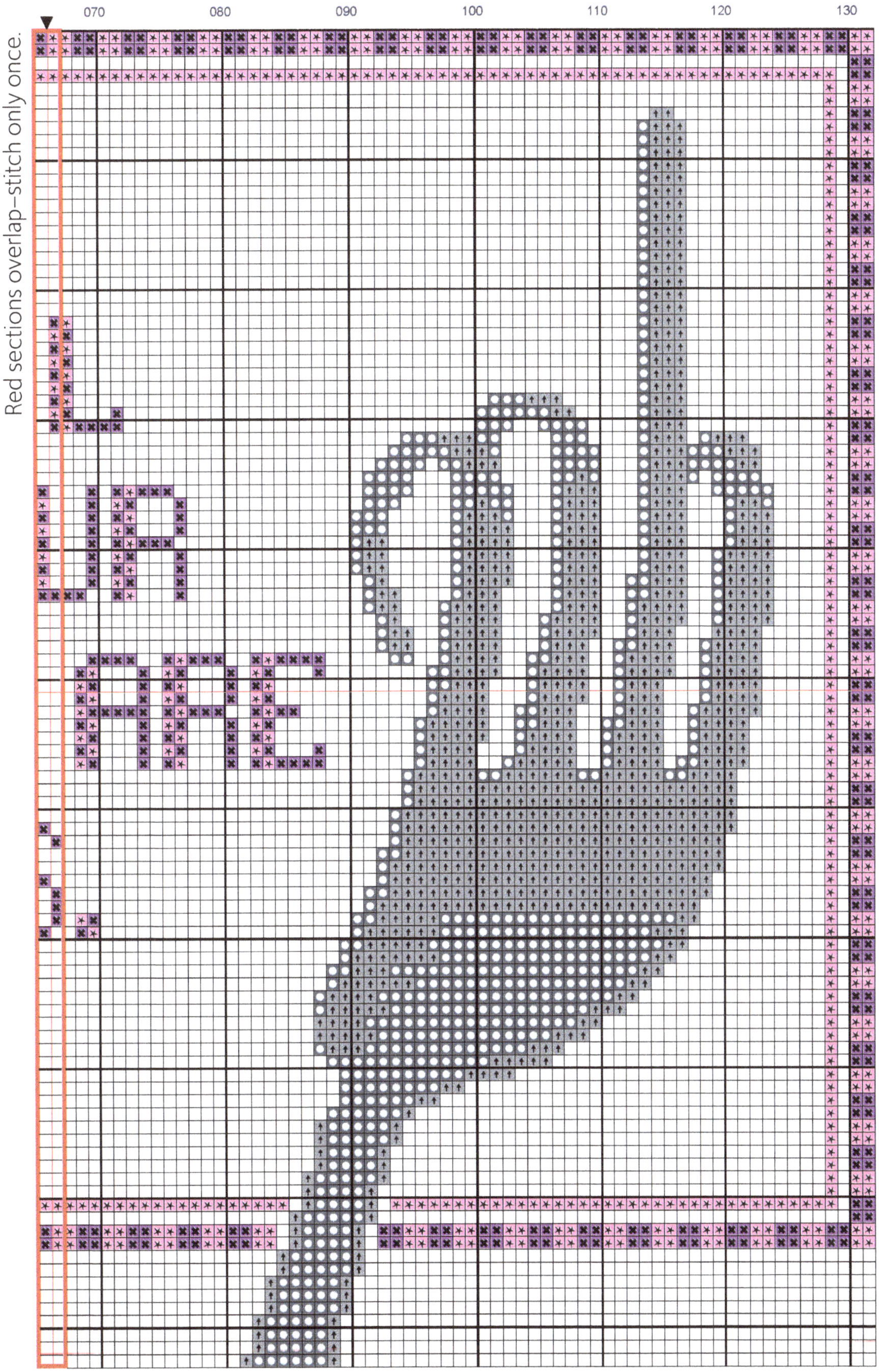

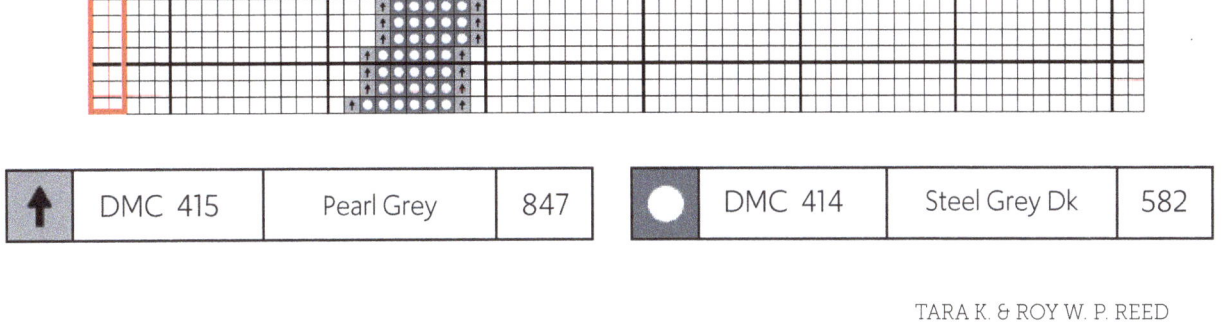

	DMC 604	Pink Mauve Lt	405
O	DMC 603	Pink Mauve Med	427
	DMC 550	Violet Very DK	489

⊙	DMC 3837	Lavender Ultra Dk	444
♥	DMC 34	Maroon Medium	371
∧	DMC 917	Plum Medium	337

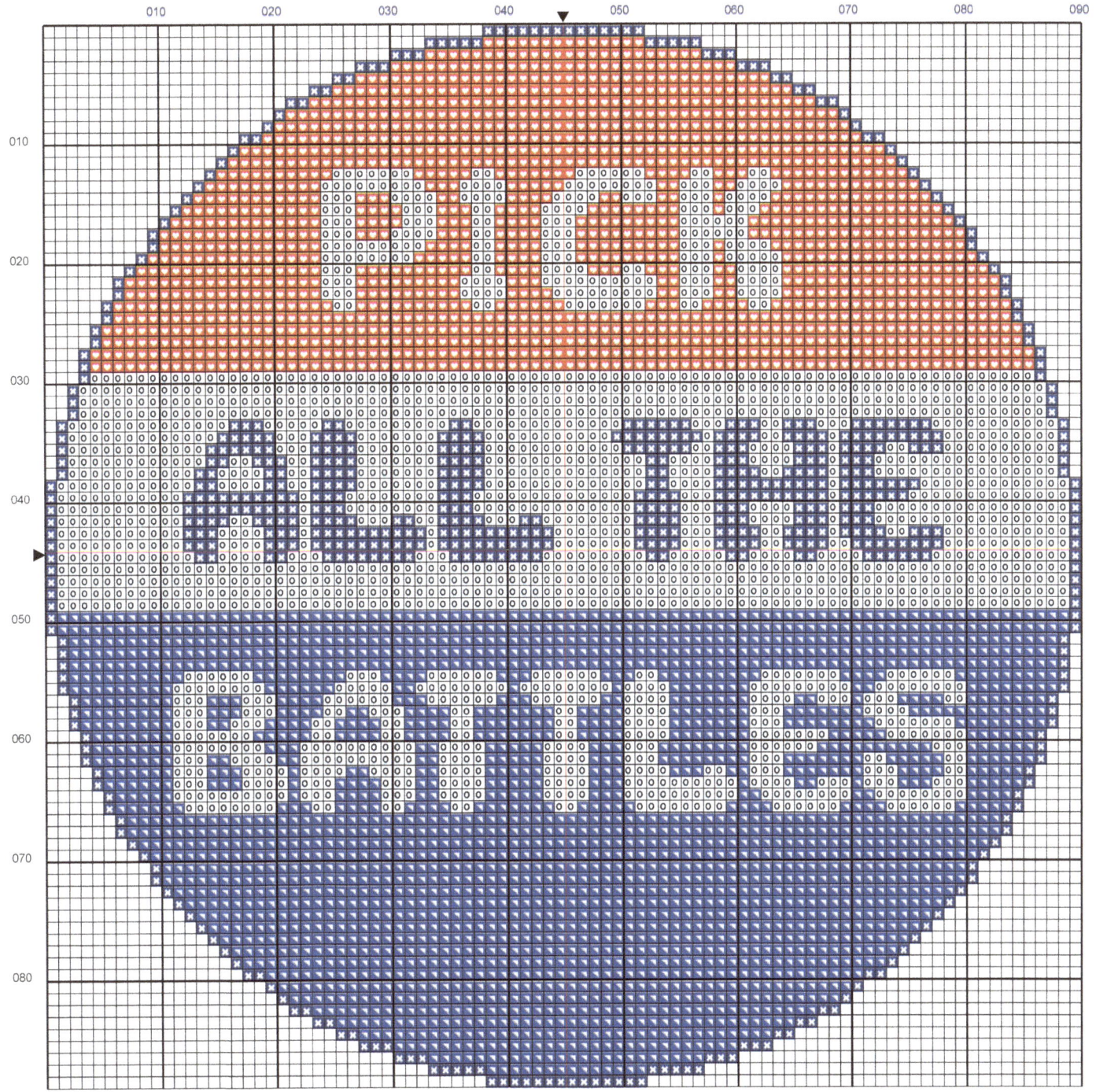

	DMC 825	Blue Dark	2177		DMC 312	Navy Blue Light	648
O	DMC B5200	Snow White	2034		DMC 666	Christmas Red Bright	1443

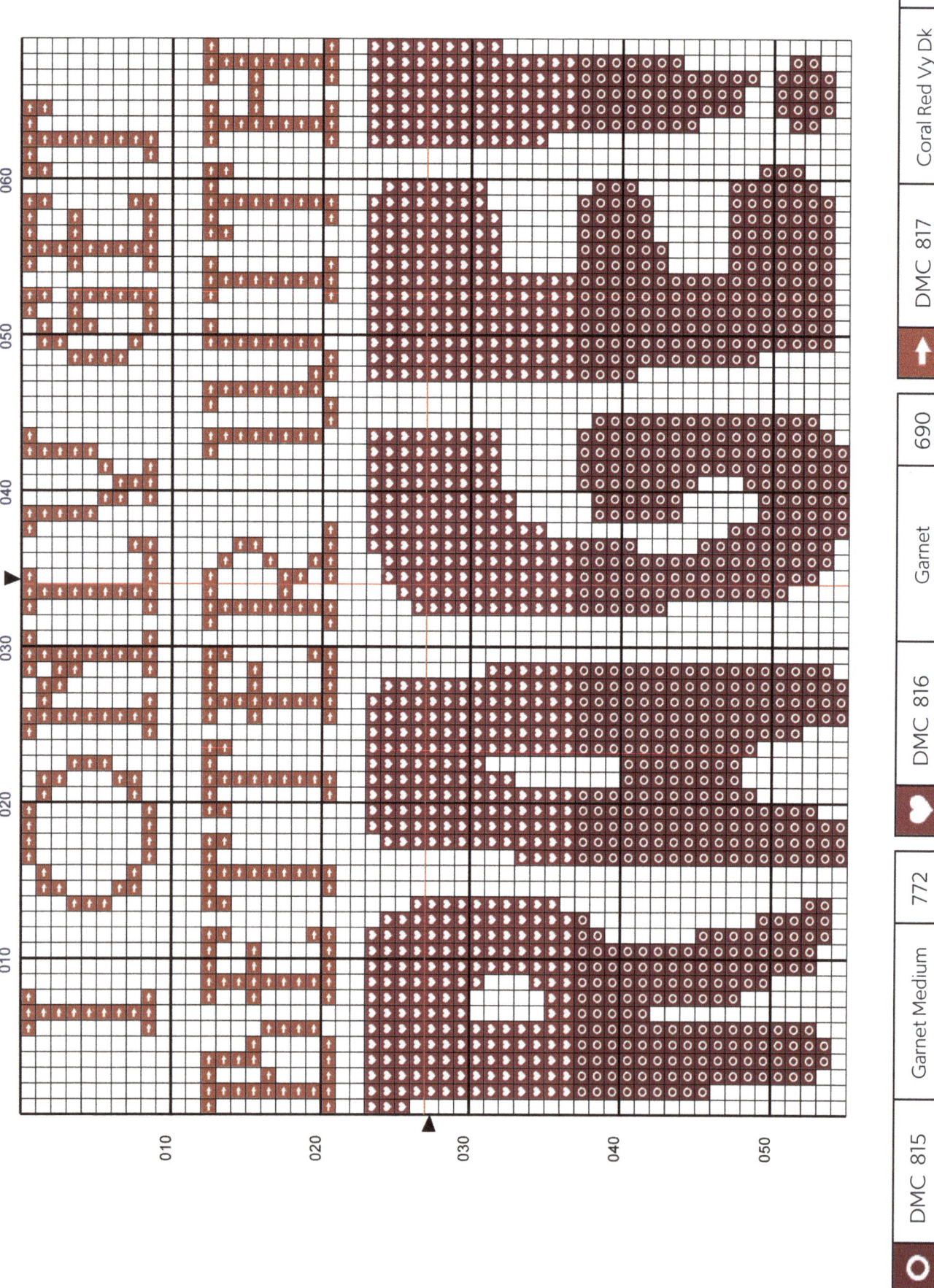

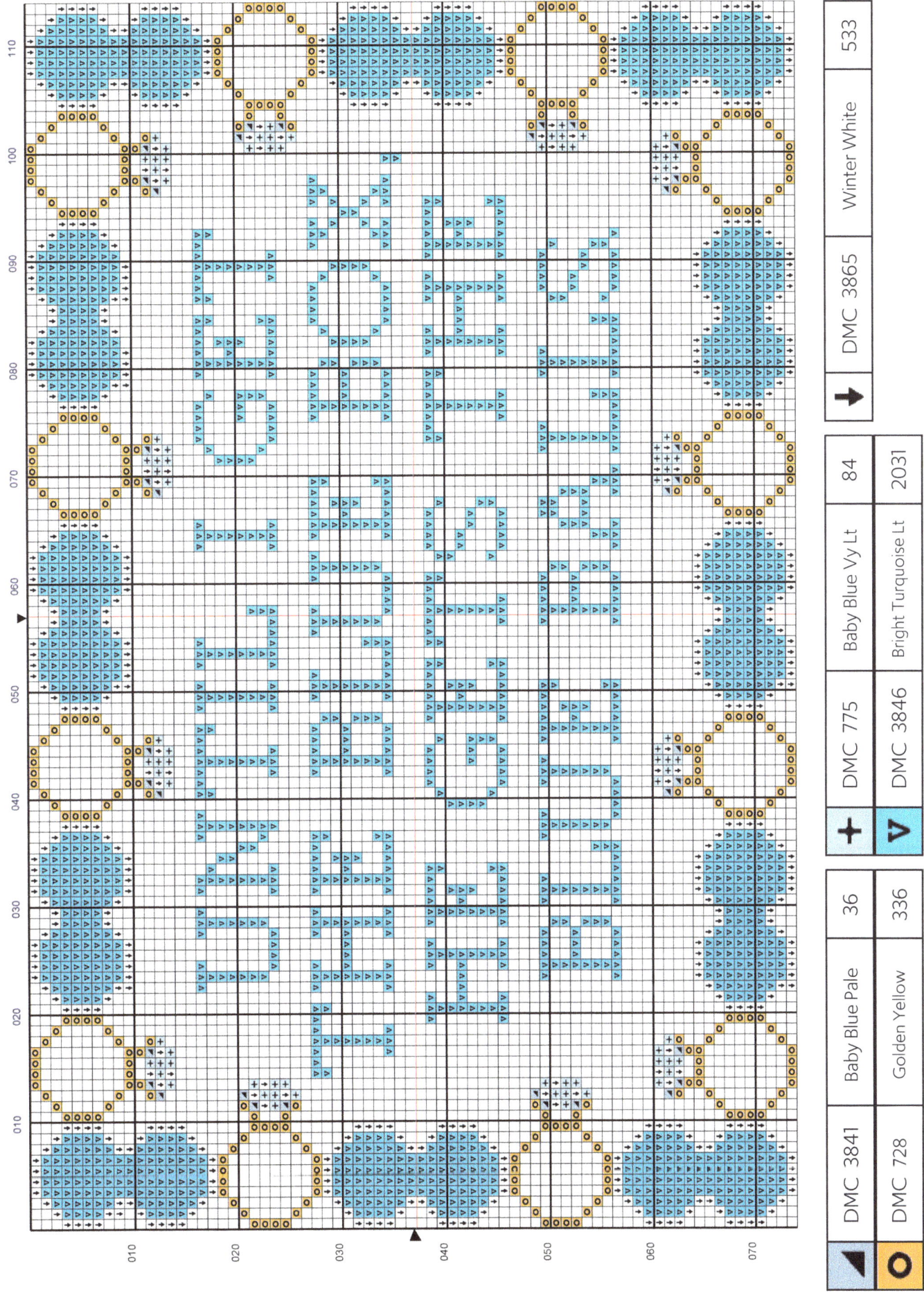

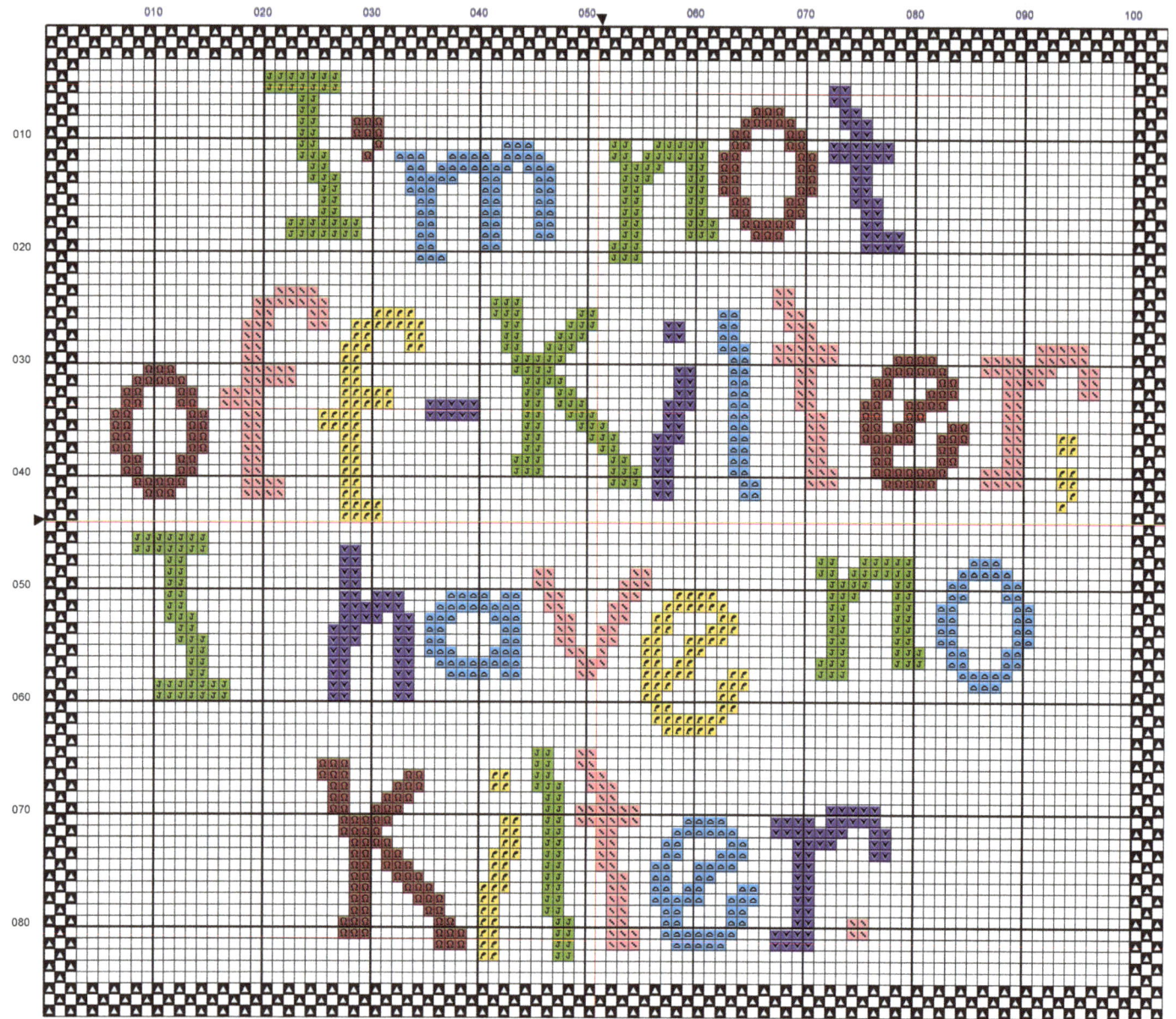

	DMC 333	Blue Violet Vy Dk	192
⌵	DMC 333	Blue Violet Vy Dk	192
⌂	DMC 996	Electric Blue Med	267
J	DMC 907	Parrot Green Lt	331
☊	DMC 726	Topaz Light	172

	DMC 3326	Rose Light	252
⋰	DMC 3326	Rose Light	252
Ω	DMC 3831	Raspberry Dark	245
▲	DMC 310	Black	555

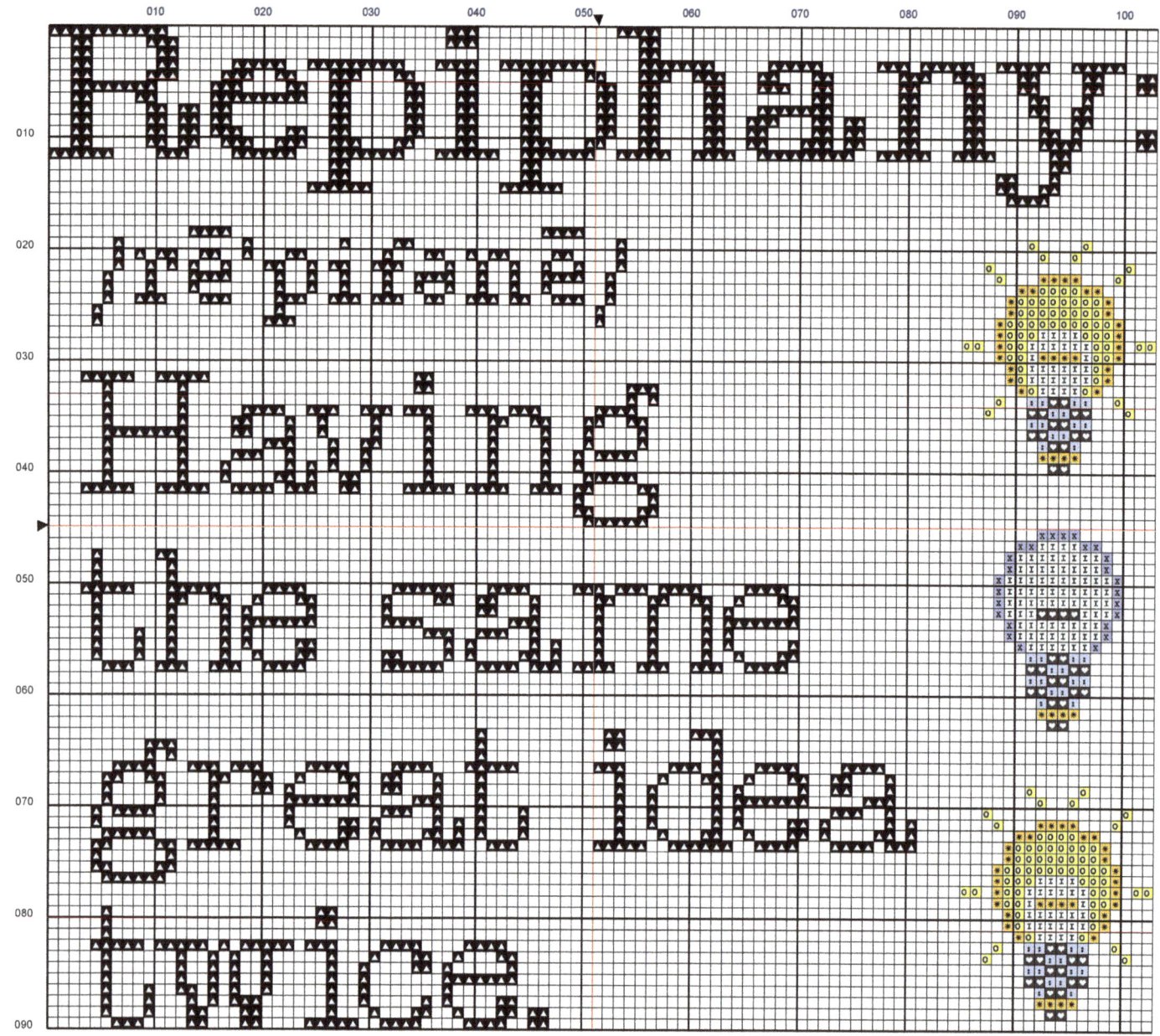

	DMC 3747	Blue Violet Vy Lt	42
♥	DMC 535	Ash Grey Vy Lt	52
▲	DMC 310	Black	1358
I	DMC 3865	Winter White	134

	DMC 341	Blue Violet Lt	26
O	DMC 445	Lemon Light	132
✻	DMC 444	Lemon Dark	72

	DMC 702	Kelly Green	291		DMC 498	Christmas Red Dk	136
	DMC 321	Christmas Red	217		DMC 701	Christmas Green Lt	160
	DMC 728	Golden Yellow	86		DMC 444	Lemon Dark	98

	DMC 310	Black	898		DMC 604	Pink Mauve Light	15
	DMC 5200	White Bright	8		DMC 603	Pink Mauve Med	568
	DMC 3854	Autumn Gold Med	377		DMC 445	Lemon Light	181

◉	DMC 3837	Lavender Ulta Dk	443	?	DMC 351	Coral	447
↑	DMC 3607	Plum Light	16	☐	DMC 307	Lemon	928
☾	DMC 550	Violet Very Dark	1277	T	DMC 327	Violet	27

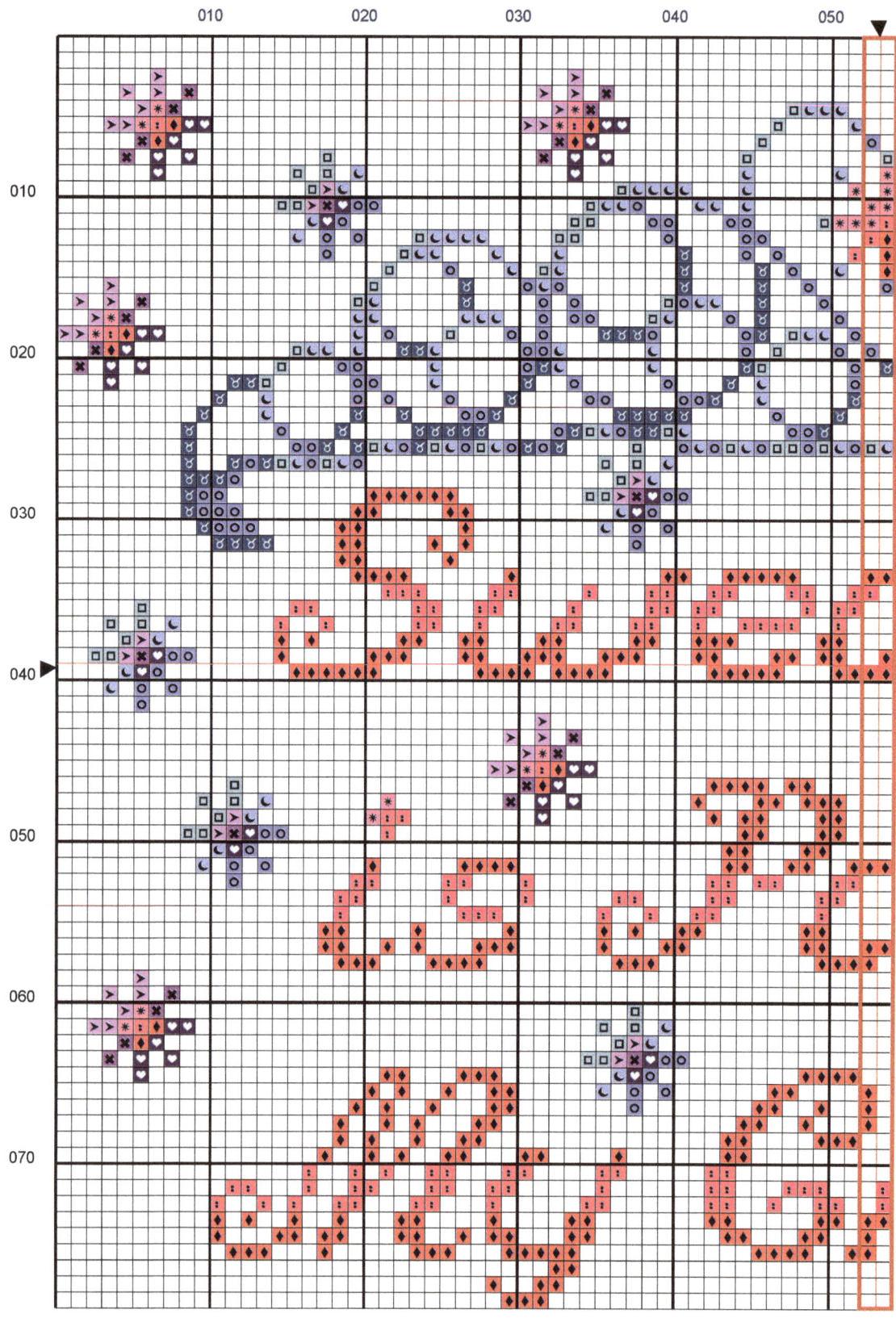

	DMC 891	Carnation Dark	535		DMC 550	Violet Very Dark	86
	DMC 893	Carnation Light	267		DMC 553	Violet	54
	DMC 957	Geranium Pale	34				

	DMC 554	Violet Light	86		DMC 3841	Baby Blue Pale	139
	DMC 341	Blue Violet Light	170		DMC 3842	Wedgewood Dark	141
	DMC 156	Blue Violet Med	212				

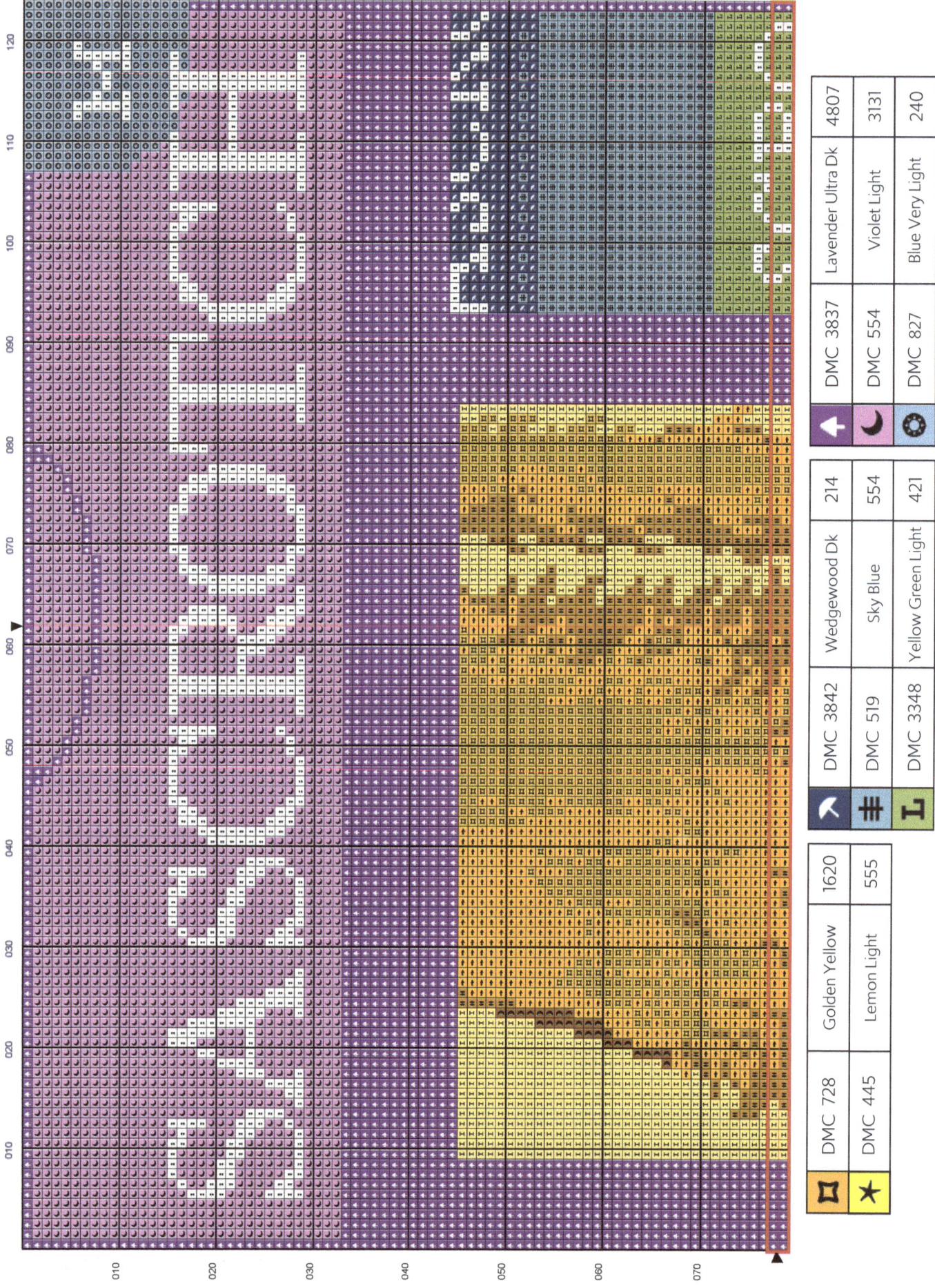

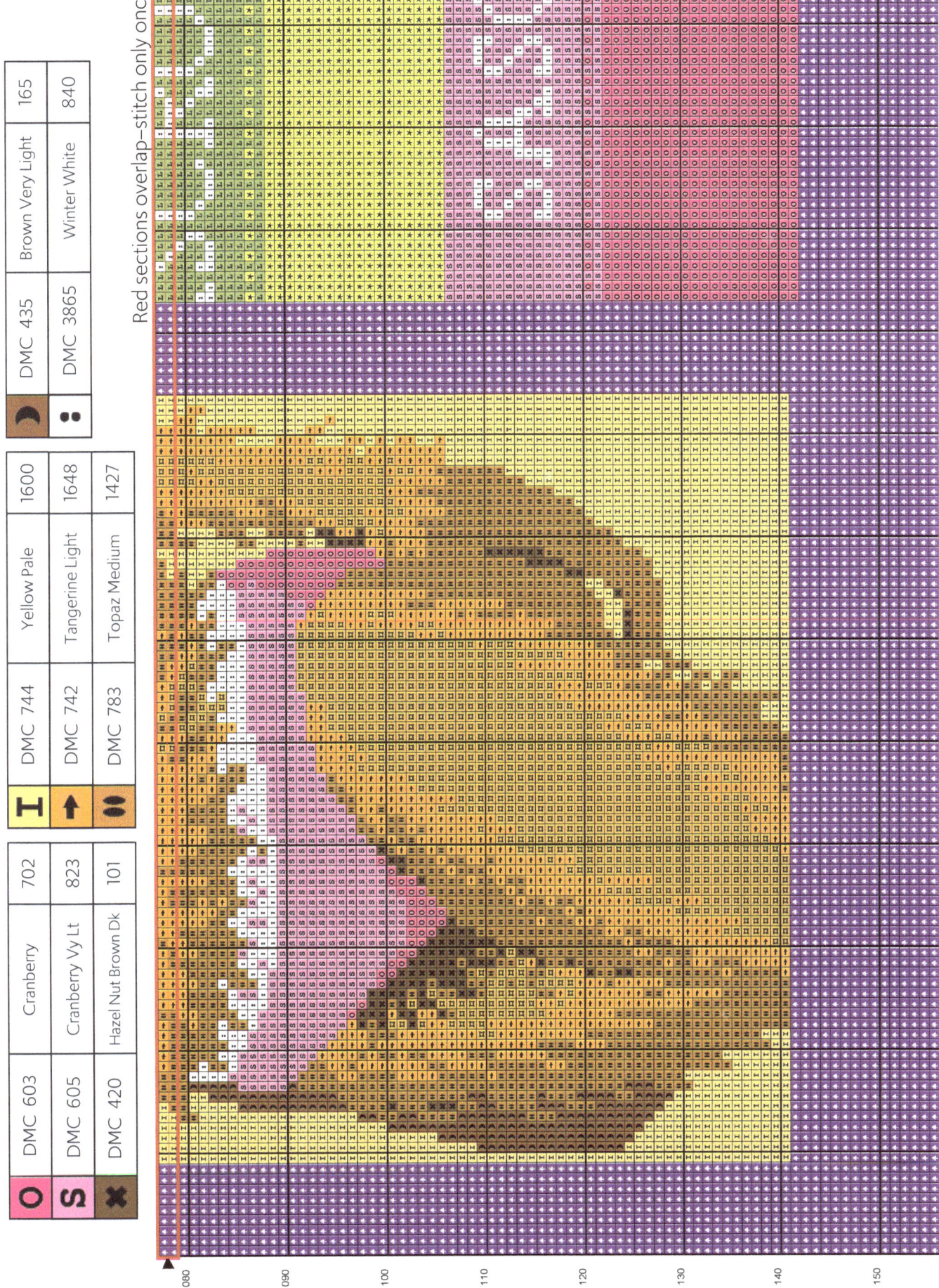

Symbol	DMC	Name	Count
✱	DMC 823	Navy Blue Dk	182
♣	DMC 3747	Blue Violet Vy Dk	479
@	DMC 3371	Black Brown	167
ʊ	DMC 3024	Brown Grey Vy Lt	382
◉	DMC 900	Burnt Orange Dk	94
#	DMC 762	Pearl Grey Vy Lt	290
S	DMC 817	Coral Red Vy Dk	354
▪	DMC 3803	Mauve Medium	240
>	DMC 726	Topaz Light	360

66 ABIT Stitches

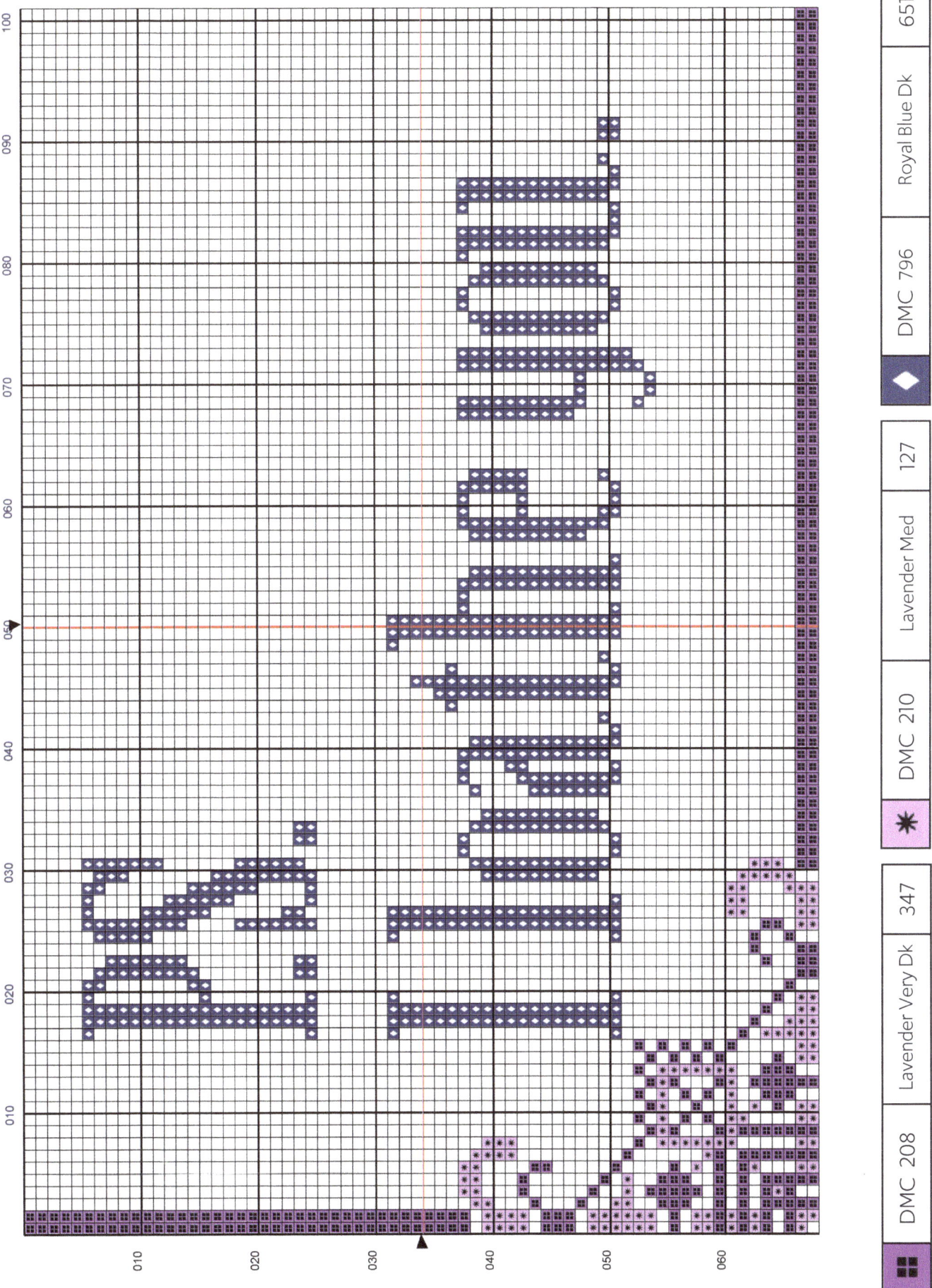

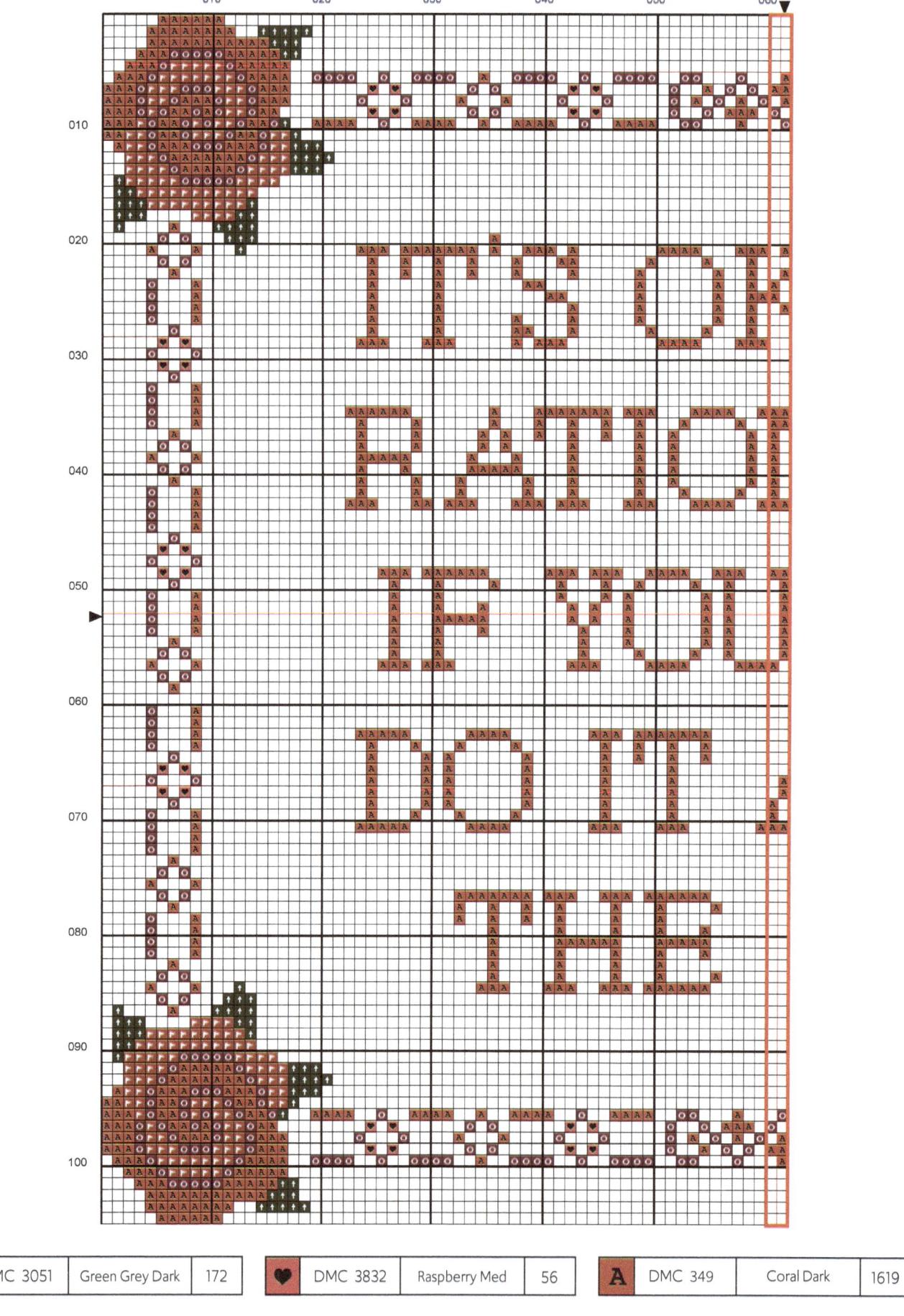

68 ABIT Stitches

Using This Book

Catalogue

Flip through the catalogue to choose your next hilarious project. Each page shows you the finished design and this mega-important information:

▲ Difficulty level (Beginner, Intermediate, Advanced)

▲ The page number(s) where you'll find the pattern chart

▲ The finished dimensions of the stitch

▲ How much aida cloth you'll need

▲ Suggested frame sizes

▲ Tips for customizing the design to your tastes

Things to note

The difficulty level is based on the total number of stitches in the design, how many colours are used, how dense the stitching is, and whether it requires backstitching. If you've never done cross-stitch before, we recommend you start with the *Beginner* designs. Once you can follow a pattern and can make uniform, tidy stitches, try the more challenging projects.

The project dimensions are given as length first, then height. They are in both metric and imperial. All measurements are based on using 14 count(ct) aida cloth. If you are using a different thread count cloth, the given dimensions will need to be adapted. There is a more detailed explanation of thread count in the **How-To** section.

The cloth estimates should guarantee that you have lots of extra material to fit your work into your embroidery hoop and a frame.

The suggested frame sizes are all available from large craft stores. They are close, not perfect matches. Custom framing is another opportunity to put your personal touch on your work.

For most of these designs, the colours used were chosen just because we like them. Our suggestions for ways to customize a pattern are only there to guide you. Feel free to play with

Put 'em on your hips instead of on your lips.

Intermediate
Pg 44
4 ¾" x 5" / 13 x 12.7cm
Aida 9" x 9" / 22.9 x 22.9cm
Frame: 6" x 6"
The coloured paper in the tray can be changed to a muted green to contrast with the red lettering. Pale blue squares will make the fries pop.
22

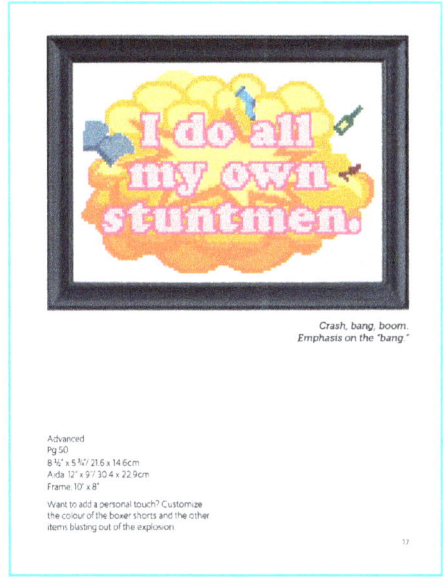

Crash, bang, boom. Emphasis on the "bang."

Advanced
Pg 50
8 ½" x 5 ¾" / 21.6 x 14.6cm
Aida 12" x 9" / 30.4 x 22.9cm
Frame: 10" x 8"
Want to add a personal touch? Customize the colour of the boxer shorts and the other items blasting out of the explosion.
17

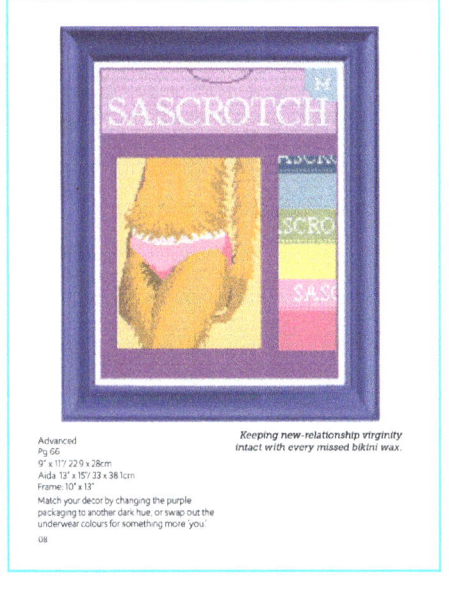

Keeping new-relationship virginity intact with every missed bikini wax.

Advanced
Pg 66
9" x 11" / 22.9 x 28cm
Aida 13" x 15" / 33 x 38.1cm
Frame: 10" x 13"
Match your decor by changing the purple packaging to another dark hue, or swap out the underwear colours for something more 'you'.
08

colour, floss type, and specialty stitches to make the designs suit your style and needs.

The specific DMC colour numbers and names used in the designs are listed on the pattern pages themselves.

Patterns

Patterns consist of two parts: thread colour tables and charts.

Each colour table tells you the number and name of the DMC colours used in each pattern. Lt=Light, Dk=Dark, Med=Medium, Vy=Very.

They also tell you the total number of stitches you will sew with each colour. This number will help you estimate how much floss you will need to buy for a project. The amount depends on what size aida cloth you are using and how many mistakes have to be ripped out. There is an estimation guide in the How-To section.

Each DMC floss listed is paired with a coloured square and a special symbol such as a heart, arrow, or star. Each coloured square represents a single stitch of the design.

Charts shows you the location of the stitches in the design and what colour thread you should use to make them. Charts are arranged in a grid system of thick and thin lines. The thick lines divide the chart into large blocks. Each large block holds 100 small stitch squares.

Charts are marked with one horizontal and one vertical red line. These lines show you where the centre of the design is, which is great because the middle is the best place to start stitching. If you try to start at an edge or corner, you could accidentally run out of room or not have enough fabric on one side of the pattern to frame it properly. **Don't sew the red centre lines into the design.**

Larger charts have been spread over two pages. This was done so the squares and symbols are as big and easy to read as possible. Each half of the chart shows a section of the design that overlaps between the two pages. Use the overlap to see how the stitches on one page connect to the stitches on the other. These sections are marked with a thick, red rectangle.

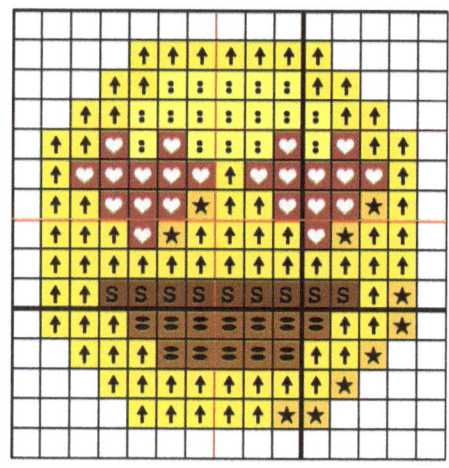

↑	DMC 307	Lemon	98
♥	DMC 321	Christmas Red	22
★	DMC 444	Lemon Dark	6
⁞	DMC 445	Lemon Light	5
S	DMC 780	Topaz Ultra Vy Dk	9
≡	DMC 782	Topaz Dark	5

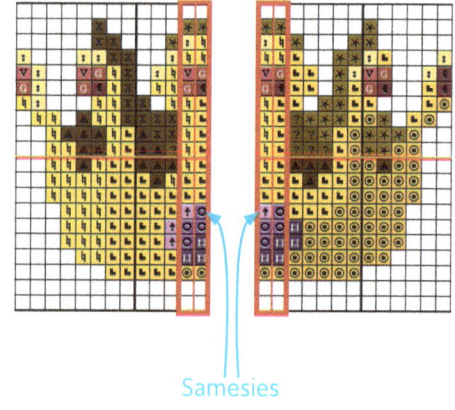

Samesies

⌑	DMC 550	⁞	DMC 745
O	DMC 552	☾	DMC 777
↑	DMC 554	G	DMC 812
V	DMC 601	▲	DMC 829
ɧ	DMC 726	X	DMC 830
⊙	DMC 728	?	DMC 831
ʟ	DMC 743	✶	DMC 832

The patterns always overlap in the middle. You only stitch the pattern contained in the red rectangle once. **You don't sew the red rectangle into your design.**

All the patterns were tested by cross-stitchers and every attempt was made to correct errors. If you do find a mistake, please contact us at TheReedStudio@gmail.com so that the design can be fixed for the next book printing.

How-To

Reading a Chart

Each square on the chart matches a square on your aida cloth. On the shoe chart, you see a row of 7 Dk pink stitches and 3 more going up at an angle. So, you sew a horizontal row of 7 stitches and 3 going up at an angle on your cloth.

Use the stitches you've already made to figure out where to place the next ones. Here, there are 3 Med pink stitches to the left side of the 3 Dk pink stitches.

Counting Stitches

Use the thick lines of the large blocks to help you count how many stitches you need to make. Each large block is 10 stitches wide and 10 stitches tall. Look at the numbered rows in the peach example. The first row has 3 Dk orange squares to the left of the thick line, and 3 more to the right. That's 6 in total. The fifth row looks like there is a lot to count, but you can see that between the two thick lines there are 2 white squares and the rest are Dk orange. Since there are 10 squares in a row, and 2 are white, then there are 8 Dk orange (10-2=8). Since there are 8 Dk orange squares in this row, there must be 7 in the row below it, because it is 1 square shorter (8-1=7).

Materials

Aida Cloth

Aida cloth is a material specifically designed for cross-stitching. Its criss-crossing weave of threads forms obvious squares with large corner holes for you to stab.

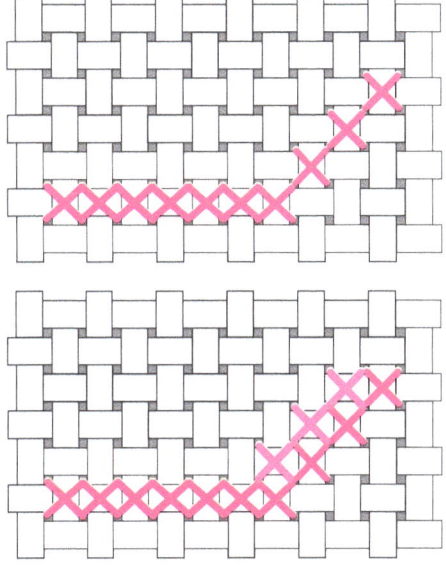

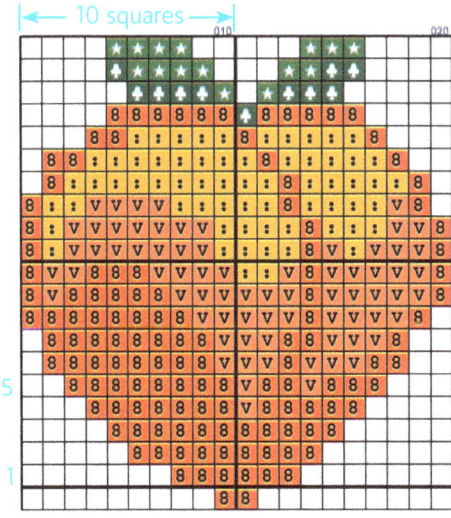

Again, all the projects in this book were designed for 14ct aida cloth. This means you have 14 stitches for every inch of fabric. A pattern that is 2 inches wide would have 28 stitches per row.

There are other counts of cloth such as 11 and 18. 11ct has 11 stitches per inch and 18ct has 18 stitches per inch. The higher the number, the more stitches you can fit in an inch.

11ct is easier for beginners, for people with poor eyesight, and those who have fine motor difficulties, because the squares and holes are bigger. 11ct uses a bigger needle, too, which might be easier to hold.

If you choose to use 11ct to make these projects, your final measurements will be a lot bigger and the recommended fabric/frame sizes won't work. You will need to convert them.

For example, a design 100 stitches long, on 14ct fabric, will have a finished stitch length of about 7 inches (100 ÷ 14 = 7.14in). The final stitch area for the same pattern on 11ct would be almost 9 inches long (100 ÷ 11 = 9.09in), so you would have to add at least two inches to the recommended length and height of your cloth. You would also need more floss because, even though you're making the same number of stitches, each individual stitch is bigger on 11ct. Finally, you might need to find a rare frame size to mount the finished piece.

Likewise, you can shrink the final dimensions by stitching on 18ct or higher. High-count aida is only recommended for advanced stitchers. It is often used for very detailed work like converted photographs that look best when stitched with little crosses. Some of the designs in this book may be too dense for 18ct if you are not an experienced stitcher.

Aida comes in different colours, too. These projects were designed for bright white fabric. If you choose an antique or off-white cloth, floss colours might look off. Some stitch colours might even blend in with the background fabric and disappear. The exception would be designs like 'Climb Every Mountain'. This project is very dense with every square stitched, so you won't necessarily see the background fabric except at the outside edges. 'Passive Aggressive' would be best on black cloth so white doesn't peek out through your black stitches.

Aida cloth can be purchased in small, pre-cut sizes or cut off of bolts found at your local sewing supply store.

74   ABIT Stitches

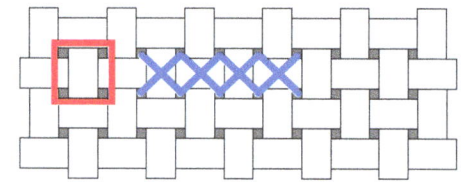

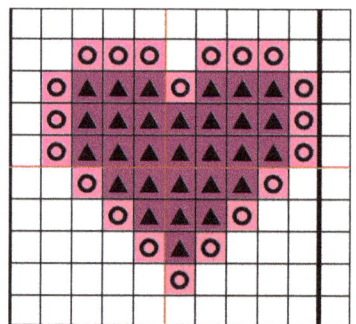

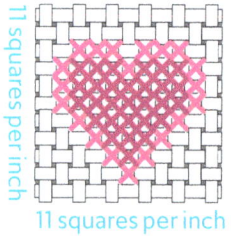

11 squares per inch

14 squares per inch

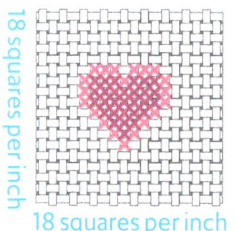

18 squares per inch

Floss

These projects were designed using the DMC colour palette. If you have a different brand of floss, you can find websites that let you convert one palette to another.

We do not recommend trying to match threads by comparing floss bundles to the colours printed in the book. There is no guarantee that the printing process didn't alter the colours on the page slightly. Every design was stitched in real life to test the colour combinations, so as long as you follow the given numbers, you will get great results, even if the piece doesn't quite match the printed page.

DMC floss generally comes in 8m/8.7yd bundles. The floss is actually 6 intertwined strands of thread, and it must be separated to use it. Our patterns were designed for 2 strands of floss at a time—each stitch is 2 strands thick.

How much floss you need greatly depends on how efficient you are and how many mistakes you make. Sewing with 2 strands on 14ct gets between 1600 to 1800 stitches per skein. If you are a beginner, figure on 1600. This chart shows our suggestion for the minimum amount of floss you'll need based on the stitch count for any given colour.

	Stitch count	Stitch range	Min. floss
Hazel Nut Brown Dk	101	Under 400 sts	1/4 skein
Tangerine Light	702	400-800 sts	1/2 skein
Topaz Medium	840	800-1200 sts	3/4 skein
Cranberry Vy Lt	1427	1200-1600 sts	full skein

Needles

Cross-stitch is usually done with tapestry needles. Unlike sewing needles, tapestry needles have fairly blunt tips that easily find their way into the holes in the aida fabric. Their eyes are much wider, so you can use multiple strands of thread at once. The most common needle sizes used for cross-stitch are 24 or 26. If you can't find ones labelled with a specific size, just keep in mind that a needle has to fit easily into the holes of the weave and you need thinner needles for higher-count cloth. Directions for threading a needle and hiding the ends of thread are in the **Step by Step** section.

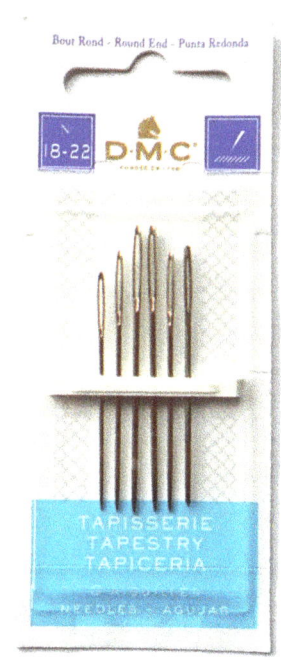

Hoops

Embroidery hoops come in many different sizes. Any hoop will do in a pinch, but one that fits most of the design inside the circular frame is best. If your hoop is too small, you will need to constantly remount the fabric. This is time-consuming and it can cause wear on your finished stitches. If the hoop is too big, you can't stretch the cloth properly, leaving floppy gaps between the fabric and the hoop

Hoops are sized by their diameter, so if you use one that is slightly larger than the longest edge of the finished project, you will have plenty of room to stitch and you won't need to reposition very often. A 6 or 8in hoop will do ya for the small projects in this collection. The large designs will fit in an 8 or 10in hoop. Directions for mounting a hoop are in the Step by Step section.

Other Tools and Materials

Besides the materials and tools described above, you'll need a ruler, pencil (or other way to mark your fabric, such as chalk or fading fabric marker), scissors and maybe a seam ripper.

Step by Step

Cut the Cloth

Each Catalogue page tells you the minimum amount of 14ct aida cloth you will need. You can alway have more than this.

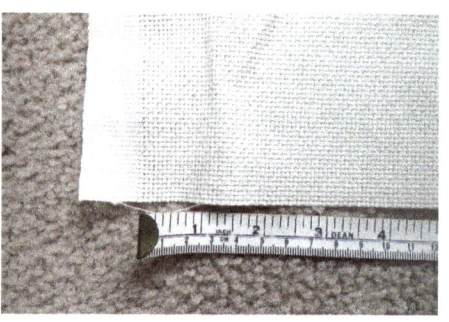

Measure from a corner of the cloth and mark the length on the edge of the fabric. Working from a corner makes sure the leftover scrap cloth is as big as possible. Scraps can be used for small projects like bookmarks. Draw a vertical and horizontal line across the fabric at your marks. The grid of the weave makes it easy to keep your pencil on track. If Danger is your middle name, cut freehand using the weave as your guide.

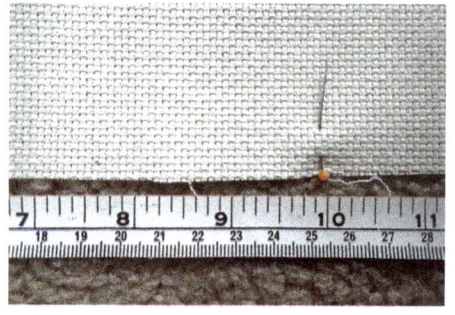

Find the Middle

Fold the aida cloth in half from left to right and press firmly on the folded edge to crease it. Open the fabric up and fold it in half from bottom to top. Crease that fold. Open it up. Mark a hole close to where the two creases criss-cross. Note the red lines on charts don't cross on a square, they cross at a hole.

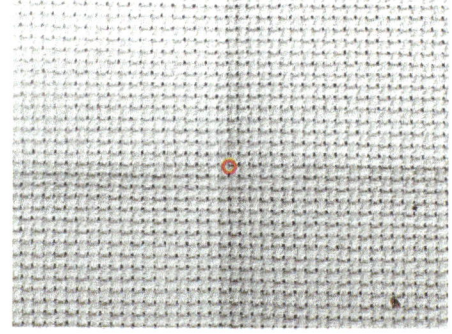

ABIT Stitches

Mount the Hoop

Unscrew the clamp until it's loose enough to separate the two rings. Place the inside ring on a clean, flat surface and lay your cloth overtop, making sure that the middle of the cloth is in the middle of the ring. Then slide the outside ring down over the cloth to trap it between the inside and outside rings. Tighten the screw clamp just slightly and pull down evenly on the edges of the cloth, rotating the hoop as you go until the middle of the cloth is taught like a drum skin and no longer shifts when tugged. Tighten the screw completely.

Be careful not to stretch completed stitches out of shape or to pull out thread ends when repositioning the hoop.

Prepare Your Floss

To separate your threads, first cut a length of floss from the bundle. If you're using 2 separate strands, cut no more than 2 feet or half a meter. If you're using one folded thread, cut no more than 1yd or 1m. Long threads get tangled. An arm-length is a good guide.

Take one end of the cut floss and fluff it with your fingers, making the individual strands spread out. Pinch one strand with one hand and pinch the rest with the other. Pull the threads apart a few inches at a time, moving your fingers down to the V where they join. Let the floss hang in the air as you pull the threads so the ends can twirl and spin freely—this prevents tangling. Explore other methods on the web if this proves too tricky.

Wrap the rest of your floss and the extra strands on a pre-punched card like the one here in the photo. These can be bought separately or as part of a floss storage kit. Label the card with the thread number so you don't mix it up with other similar shades. You could store all the colours for one project on a keyring.

TARA K. & ROY W. P. REED

Thread the Needle

There are many different methods to thread your needle. Here are a few. They each have advantages and disadvantages. It comes down to personal preference.

Double strands: Line up one end of each strand and push them both through the eye of the needle, pulling about 1 foot/30 cm through the eye. This extra prevents the needle from falling off. Don't tie any knots yet. As you stitch, slide the needle farther up the thread until you only have a couple of inches left. This method works for any number of strands and you can just slip the needle off and thread it back on when you're done pulling. Use the **Knot** or **Weave** method to secure your thread to your work (see below).

Single Strand (Version 1): Thread one end through the needle and pull exactly half the thread through the eye. Line up the ends. Don't tie any knots yet. Use the **Knot** or **Weave** method to secure your thread to your work (see below).

Single Strand (Version 2): This is a combo of the first two methods. Fold the strand in half exactly and thread the cut ends through the needle. Pull about half a foot/15cm through the eye. No knots yet. This method has the same advantage of slipping the needle off and on when you make mistakes. Use the **Loop Method** to secure your thread (see below).

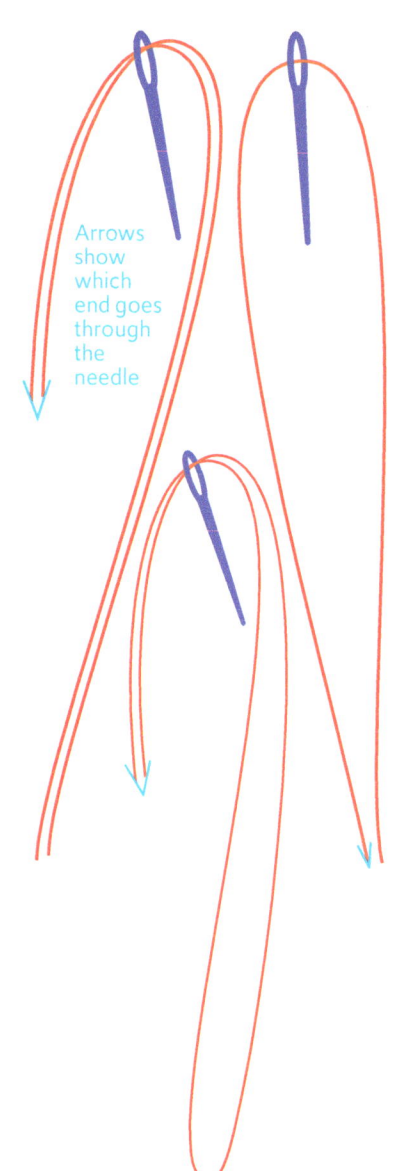

Start Stitching

Find Your Starting Point

Pick a section near the middle of the chart (the two red lines cross). Choose an area with a group of the same colour if you can. In this example, the first stitch is going to be the far left end of the top red row. That stitch is 10 squares to the left and 3 squares up from the middle of the pattern. So, look at the centre mark on your aida cloth. Count 10 squares to the left and 3 squares up from your mark (see the blue star). That square is going to be where your first stitch goes. Mark that first square.

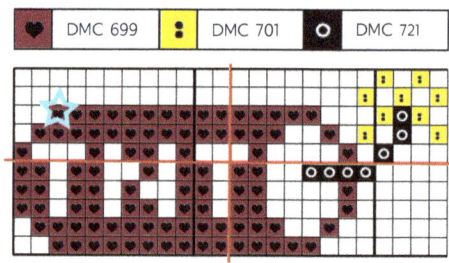

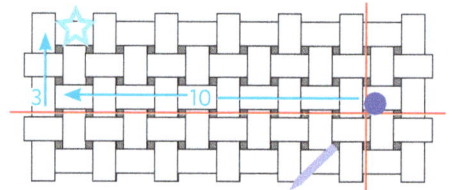

Secure Your Thread

You have to secure the loose end of your thread or it will unravel and you'll lose stitches.

Knot Method: This is the easiest but not the prettiest or most effective method. Tie the ends of your threads several times to make a large knot. Make it big enough that it won't pop through the hole in your aida cloth. You can use reef knots (like when tying shoes) tied close together.

Position your needle at the back of your hoop, locating the top-left hole of the square you marked. Push your needle through to the front and pull the thread all the way out until the knot snags against the hole. If the knot pops out, you have to make it bigger.

Weave Method: This is a fairly advanced technique but it is very neat and tidy, and highly recommended. This is our variation on a standard method.

Choose an area to start where you will be stitching at least 4 stitches in a row. Mark the square you're starting with (see green star to the right). From the front of the aida cloth, count 4 squares to the right of your marked stitch. Push the needle through the bottom-right hole of the 4th square. Pull the thread until a tail about 1in/2cm sticks out of the top of the fabric. Smooth the tail out so it points to the right. Carry the thread across the back to your first stitch and start stitching as normal. Hold down the tail with one hand and pull the thread until you feel the tail tugging. Stitch all the first strokes of this row. As you work, each stitch is wrapping around the tail at the back of the cloth. Trim the extra bit of tail sticking out from the front. Continue your stitches as you would normally.

If you already have rows of stitches near your starting point, slip the needle underneath the backside of 4 or 5 stitches and pull the thread through until the end is trapped. Then push the needle through the top-left hole of your starting square.

Loop Method: Using Single Strand (Version 2) threading method, start your first stitch as normal. Pull the thread out until about 1in/2cm of the looped end is left sticking out the back of the cloth. Complete the first stitch through the bottom-right hole and pull the thread all the way without yanking the loop free. Feed the needle through the looped end. Pull the thread until the looped end tightens around the length of thread. Don't pull too tight or you could misshape the square and leave a gap. Continue stitching as you would normally.

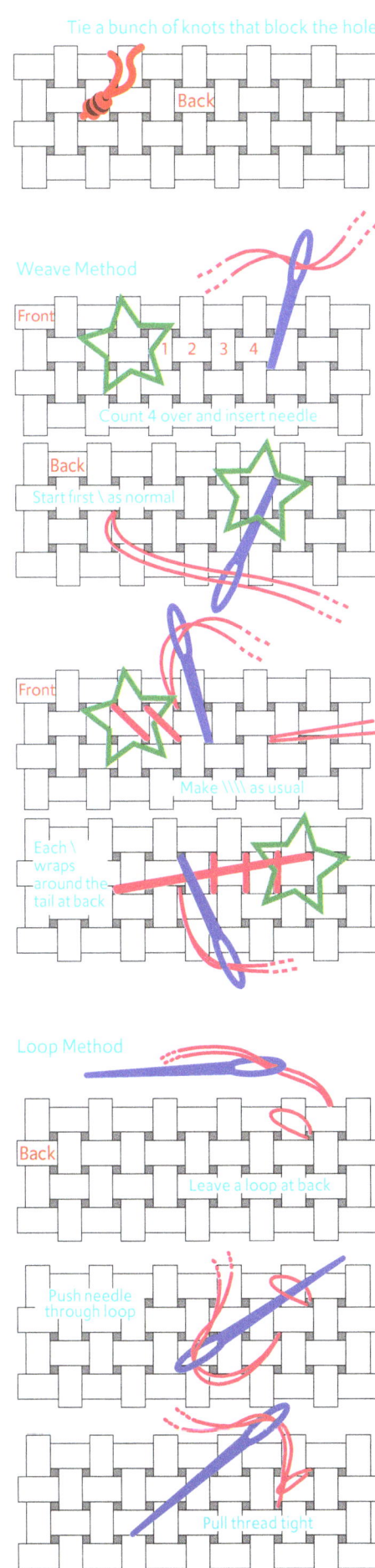

Stitch a Row

Contrary to how it looks, cross-stitching is not done by making X after X all over the fabric. You do so for random details like flowers in a field, but if you are stitching grouped areas, there is a more efficient and tidy way to it.

Your work will look crisper and more polished if all of your stitches are uniform. This means the top strokes all go one direction and the bottom strokes all go the opposite way.

In this example, you can see the first stroke of each stitch is made by pulling the needle up through the top-left hole of each square and then pushed down through the bottom-right hole. This makes a row of \\\ that all travel in the same direction. To complete the X, push the needle up through the top-right hole and down through the bottom-left hole.

This example is for stitching left-to-right. If you have to go right-to-left, come up through the bottom-right hole and go down the top-left hole to make the same \\\ strokes.

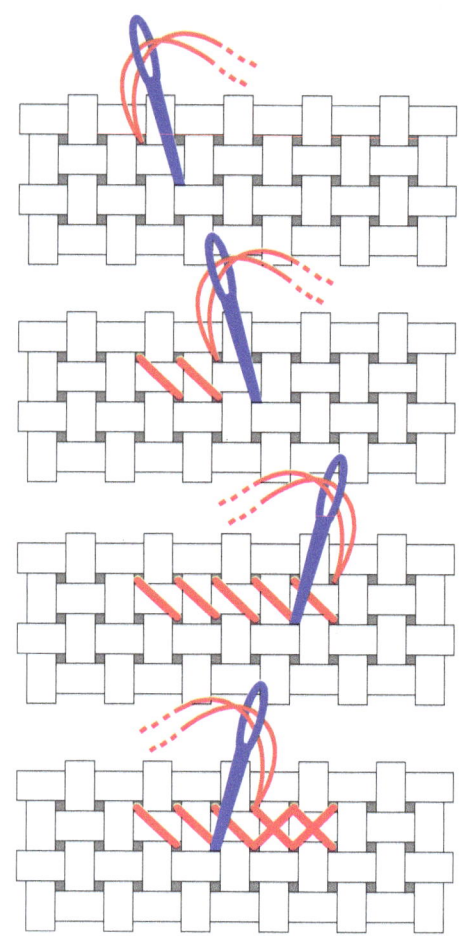

Mistakes

From time to time, you might realize you miscounted and have too many or incorrectly placed stitches. Don't panic. If you're using the open end method of threading, just pull the stitches out in reverse order of how you stitched them. Or, use your seam ripper to carefully lift each thread and gently pull up to cut them. Do one stitch at a time, slowly. Don't cut the aida cloth. This is why it's good to have extra floss.

Backstitching

Backstitches make outlines and add details. The charts only show you the outline to follow. For this example, pretend the arrows are your needle. Come up Hole 1 then go down Hole 2. Run the thread across the back so you can come up 3. Go down 4 then run the thread so you come up 5. Go down 6 and cross the back to 7. Start and end your threads as you normally would.

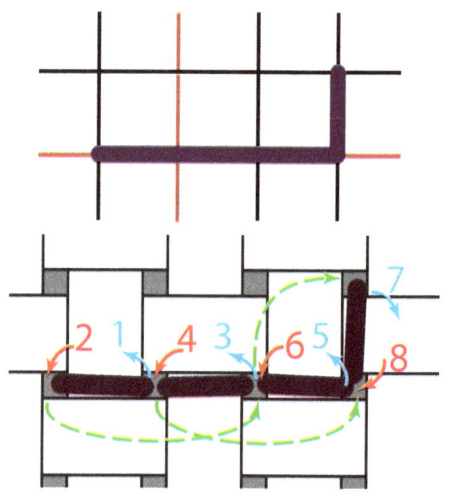

Ending a Thread

When you are down to about 2 in/5cm of thread left on your needle, slide the needle under a row of three or four stitches at the back of the work. Cut the tail so no threads poke out.

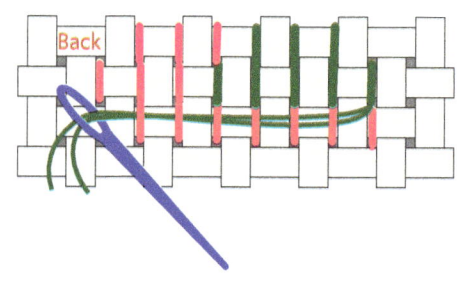

Threads criss-crossing on the back of your fabric is unavoidable, but too much can be a hassle and it wastes floss. Reduce waste by planning your stitches. When it's time to jump to another section, decide if you can save floss by ending the thread and starting fresh in a new location.

Finishing

Wrinkles and Dirt

Your finished design might be a bit wrinkled or have a smudge or two. This is easily fixed by gently hand-washing the work with lukewarm water and a few drops of a mild soap. Once clean, let the water drip away. DO NOT twist or squeeze your work. Lay the project between two fluffy towels and press gently all over. Remove the piece from the towels and lay flat to dry. Place the dry piece upside down on an ironing board and use low heat to flatten the cloth. You can put a clean piece of white or light cloth over the cross-stitch if you're worried you might burn it. Don't press hard or you could crush the stitches. Don't iron on the front, as heat can sometimes cause an unwanted shine.

Keep it clean. Store some wipes in your kit if you're on the road or if you like to snack while stitching.

Framing

The method you use for framing really depends on the kind of frame you buy.

If the frame has a backing board, fold the sides of the aida cloth around it to the back. You might need to trim the board's edges slightly if the thickness of the cloth makes it hard to fit the board back in the frame. You can make your own backing board out of the card from a cereal box.

You can also cut the fabric to the same size as the frame and sandwich the piece between the glass and the backing board. Place the frame on the piece so you can centre the design by looking through the glass and trace where to cut. A piece of mat board can hide any fraying cloth

'Revenge is the Best Revenge' can be mounted in a 6in hoop. Trim away the aida cloth so you have 1-2in/3-5cm of fabric sticking out all around the hoop. Fold this extra cloth behind the hoop and use some zigzagging whip stitches to pull all the edges together.

ABIT About Us

Tara K. Reed

When her public relations career was derailed by a sickening plot twist, Tara published her first interactive novel, 'Love Him Not'—a satirical dating adventure inspired by dozens of dating advice books and offering hundreds of realistic choices and 60 (mostly unhappy) endings. Tara is a regular blogger for Huffington Post Canada and lives in Niagara Falls with her husband and many cats.
www.Doorflower.com

Roy W. P. Reed

Roy is an elementary school teacher with 20 years of experience and expertise in math and special education. He holds Bachelors of Education and Fine Arts from Queen's University in Canada. He's a master-crafter in just about any medium, especially textiles. He has published two popular dot-to-dot and searchword books that offer children and adults a creative way to improve and maintain their math and reading skills. www.TheReedStudio.com

Erin Bennett (nee Reed)

Erin has been exploring art and design since she could hold a pencil. She studied graphic design at Humber College in Canada and has contributed to many Dot-to-Dot and cross-stitching books. She is the owner of Bitter Honey Custom Creations in London, Ontario, as well as a hairstylist and married mother of five.
www.BitterHoneyCustomCreations.com

What's that?
30 pithy patterns aren't enough for you? You're insatiable!

Fortunately, we anticipated your thirst and designed more patterns that aren't featured in this book. Want 'em? Well, you're gonna have to work for 'em. Each pattern below tells you what you need to do to receive it.

#1 Everyone in Moderation

Sign up for the ABIT Newsletter at www.ABITStitches.com! As a subscriber, you'll be notified about all ABIT products, sales and FREE stuff like this pattern!

#2 Glad you aren't here

Show us your stitches on Instagram! Post a photo of your finish from a purchased "ABIT" pattern and we'll send you this free design.

Tag @ABITStitches, @DoorflowerCo and @TheReedStudio.

DM the post to @ABITStitches along with your email address to collect your free pattern!

Read more by Tara K. Reed

To deliver yourself from evil, *turn to section 64.*

To be led into tempation, *turn to section 22.*

Are you an expert at the game of love? Find out in Love Him Not, an interactive unromantic comedy where YOU become the protagonist. As Elle Masters, you'll navigate hundreds of familiar dating dilemmas and passionate predicaments inspired by popular advice books and modern romance. Each choice is more complicated than the last, and the stakes are raised with each turn of the page, but you'll have backup from Elle's best friends, Rachel and Valerie, who put the "antics" in "romantics."

With 60 endings ranging from "I don't know what happened!" to "I do," don't be surprised if art imitates life and you throw this book across the room... only to pick it up and try again. One more time. Because, unlike real life, when you don't like the outcome, you can go back to a pivotal moment and explore the path not taken, or even start over at the beginning.

"Tara K. Reed creates a world that feels like your new favorite TV show: quick, funny, warm, populated by characters you love, love to hate, and some you'd love to...ahem...get to know very well. Plus, she makes YOU the star of these completely binge-worthy adventures. Get ready for your close-up, darling, and crack this spine." - Zageris and Curran, 'My Lady's Choosing' and 'Taylor Swift: Girl Detective'.

"'Love Him Not' possesses all those juicy traits of modern-day courtship: the support of great friends, the goosebumps over the guy, the over-thinking as intimacy grows or ebbs, and the delirium when things go right. Readers guide the loveable Elle Masters toward many futures with Mr. Wright in this fun, witty book. The author manages to find nearly every real-life situation a couple endures on the way to (potential) romantic bliss, which makes the story relatable and incredibly hard to put down." – Patience Bloom, 'Romance is My Day Job'

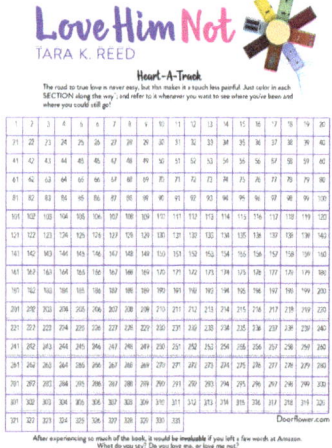

For maximum heartache, track your progress so you don't miss a single choice or ending. Visit www.Doorflower.com for a printable 'Heart-A-Track' sheet that lets you cross off each section as you go. Also get a copy of the Love Him Not 'Happy Endings' Map in case you want to skip the trials and head straight to the fibrillations!

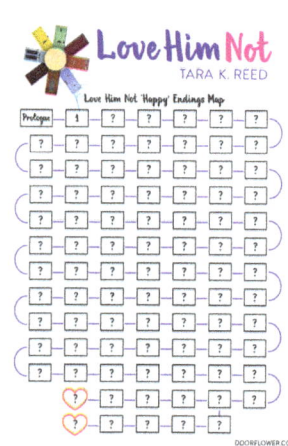

Dot to Dot to Dot

88 Advanced Dot to Dot Puzzles with Extra Dots

By Roy W. P. Reed & Erin Reed

These are extreme dot to dots. They skip-count by 1s, 2s, 3s, 4s, 5s, 6s, 7s, 8s, 9s, and 10s. They begin at different starting points for even more of a challenge. And they have EXTRA DOTS!

Follow the counting pattern, skipping the extra dots to find the hidden pictures. Make a mistake, and the picture will be lost. But don't worry, that's what erasers are for.

Ice cream @ %100
Text lightened for effect
This note is 8pt font

Entertaining
- A unique twist on a popular activity
- A range of levels, challenging children 8+ and adults
- Fun all year round with seven holiday and seasonal themes
- 8pt font or larger, easier to read than other popular puzzles

Educational
- Researched-based mental math practice, created by an experienced educator
- Educators are directed to a free teaching guide
- Fully reproducible for use with students

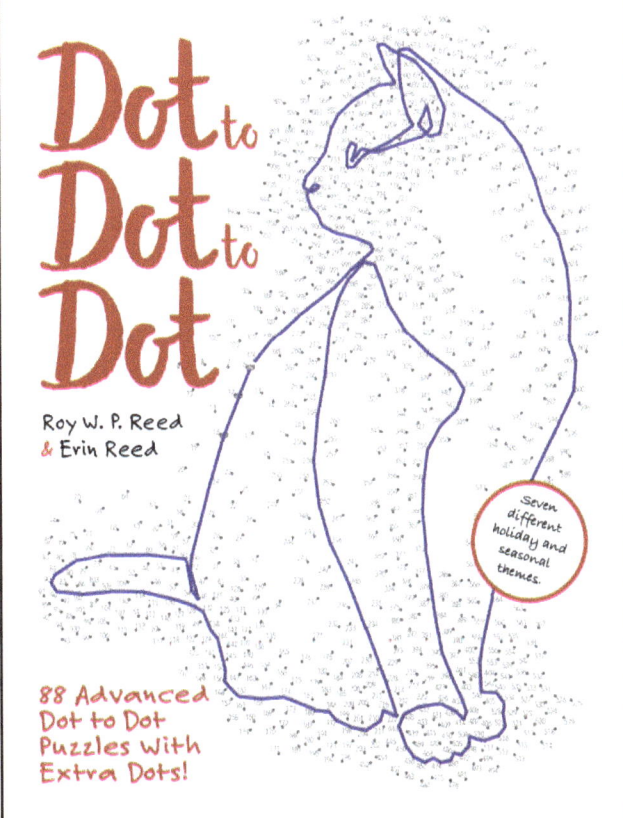

4.5 Stars on Amazon

"I love that you took a simple concept and upped the rigour!"

"Kids totally loved it!"

"I have done a few of the more challenging ones myself, and they are addictive. I hope there are some left for my daughter when she is ready for them. Great find!"

Colour Substitution Tables

ABIT gives suggestions for customizing our designs to suit your tastes. Some of those suggestions include changing the colours. Use these blank tables to keep track of your colour substitutions. Write directly in the book or photocopy the tables.

For each new colour, record the page number for the pattern you are customizing, draw the symbol for the colour you are replacing, write the original DMC number and colour name, write the new number and colour name, and write the number of stitches so you can estimate how much floss you'll need.

Page	★	Original #	Original Name	New #	New Name	# Sts
		DMC		DMC		
		DMC		DMC		
		DMC		DMC		
		DMC		DMC		
		DMC		DMC		

Page	★	Original #	Original Name	New #	New Name	# Sts
		DMC		DMC		
		DMC		DMC		
		DMC		DMC		
		DMC		DMC		
		DMC		DMC		

Page	★	Original #	Original Name	New #	New Name	# Sts
		DMC		DMC		
		DMC		DMC		
		DMC		DMC		
		DMC		DMC		
		DMC		DMC		

Page	★	Original #	Original Name	New #	New Name	# Sts
		DMC		DMC		
		DMC		DMC		
		DMC		DMC		
		DMC		DMC		
		DMC		DMC		

Page	★	Original #	Original Name	New #	New Name	# Sts
		DMC		DMC		
		DMC		DMC		
		DMC		DMC		
		DMC		DMC		
		DMC		DMC		

Page	★	Original #	Original Name	New #	New Name	# Sts
		DMC		DMC		
		DMC		DMC		
		DMC		DMC		
		DMC		DMC		
		DMC		DMC		

Page	★	Original #	Original Name	New #	New Name	# Sts
		DMC		DMC		
		DMC		DMC		
		DMC		DMC		
		DMC		DMC		
	★	DMC		DMC		

www.ingramcontent.com/pod-product-compliance
Lightning Source LLC
Chambersburg PA
CBHW061143010526
44118CB00026B/2861